The Advertising Advantage

THE ADVERTISING ADVANTAGE

A Harvard Business Review Paperback

ISBN 0-87584-280-1

The *Harvard Business Review* articles in this collection are available as individual reprints, with the exception of "Critical Issues for Issue Ads" and "Can You Pass the Comparative Ad Challenge?". Discounts apply to quantity purchases. For information and ordering, contact Operations Department, Harvard Business School Publishing Division, Boston, MA 02163. Telephone: (617) 495-6192, 9 a.m. to 5 p.m. Eastern Time, Monday through Friday. Fax: (617) 495-6985, 24 hours a day.

Editor's Note: Some articles included in this book may have been written before authors and editors began to take into consideration the role of women in management. We hope the archaic usage representing all managers as male does not detract from the usefulness of the collection.

Printed in the United States of America by Harvard University, Office of the University Publisher.
93 92   5 4 3

Contents

Comparative Advertising

Advertising Techniques

Costs and Benefits
of Advertising

SPECIAL REPORT

Too much of advertising and promotion is wasted. With single-source marketing data, it doesn't have to be.

Getting the Most Out of Advertising and Promotion

by Magid M. Abraham and Leonard M. Lodish

Until recently, believing in the effectiveness of advertising and promotion has largely been a matter of faith. Marketing departments might collect voluminous statistics on television program ratings and on coupon redemptions and carefully compare the costs of marketing with total sales. But none of this data measures what is really important: the *incremental* sales of a product over and above those that would have happened without the advertising or promotion.

Thanks to a new kind of marketing data, that situation is changing. The data correlate information on actual consumer purchases (available from universal-product-code scanners used in supermarkets and drugstores) with information on the kind of television advertising those consumers receive or the frequency and type of promotion events they see. Armed with this consumer products data from a "single source," manag-

ers can measure the incremental impact of marketing-mix variables such as advertising, merchandising, and pricing.

Forward-looking senior managers are beginning to realize that single-source data provide an unparalleled opportunity to increase their company's marketing productivity – if they know how to take advantage of it. Doing so requires developing new marketing strategies and radically redefining the responsibilities of a company's sales force.

At the strategic level, managers must evaluate marketing data differently and put incremental sales and profits into management objectives. This means continually examining the appropriate balance between advertising and promotion, based on marginal-productivity analysis.

The search for fresh, innovative television advertising to boost sales of established products should be constant. Until such advertising is

found, it may pay to cut back on advertising spending. Using single-source test markets as "lead markets" for national advertising campaigns can substantially lower the risk of this approach.

Managers must also cut back on unproductive promotions in favor of hard-to-imitate promotion events that directly contribute to incremental profitability. And they must use the new data to shape distinctive promotional efforts for specific local markets and key accounts.

In this dynamic marketing environment, the sales force will have a different and extremely important job: to demonstrate to retailers the consumer pull of its company's advertising and promotion programs, as well as the effect these programs have on retailer profitability. New strategies that benefit *both* retailer and manufacturer must replace the traditional practice of using advertising and promotion as inducements to carry a product.

Above all, senior managers must throw out much of the conventional wisdom about advertising and promotion that has formed over the years. Replacing these widely held but unsupported beliefs with marketing strategies based on hard data is the key to attaining a new kind of market power.

What's wrong with the conventional wisdom

Because they have been unable to measure the incremental sales of advertising and promotion before now, marketing managers have had to rely on a number of unexamined assumptions. For example, those who believe advertising works also tend to assume that in all cases, more of it is better than less. This assumption is frequently justified by another: that advertising takes a long time – many months or, sometimes, even years – to increase sales.

Magid M. Abraham is president of product development and marketing at Information Resources, Inc., a Chicago-based vendor of syndicated single-source data. Leonard M. Lodish is the Samuel R. Harrell Professor of Marketing at the Wharton School.

Another by-product of the traditional lack of data on incremental sales is the common belief that once advertising does start producing sales, its impact is short term. A popular rule of thumb is that if increased advertising spending does not generate enough sales to pay for the incremental expense within a year, then a company shouldn't implement the advertising.

Finally, many marketing managers will tell you that even if advertising is *not* directly boosting sales, it still

Only 16% of trade promotions are profitable – and for many, the cost of an extra $1 of sales is *greater* than $1.

serves an important function. When salespeople can point to a big ad budget, this convinces retailers that the manufacturer supports the product, thus assuring its distribution in the stores.

So too with promotions. Traditionally, the focus has been on gross rather than incremental sales. The conventional wisdom is that a successful promotion is one where a company sells a lot of goods to the trade and that a promotion for an established brand can be used to attract and retain new users of the brand. In fact, promotions have become so popular that they now account for more than 65% of typical marketing budgets.

Our research challenges all of these beliefs. Since 1982, we have been using single-source data to examine the productivity of the marketing dollar spent on advertising and promotions for consumer packaged goods. The results are striking:

□ In 360 tests in which the only variable was advertising weight – the amount of television advertising to which consumers are exposed – increased advertising led to more sales only about half the time.

□ Analyses of trade promotions for all brands in 65 different product categories suggest that the productivity of promotion spending is even worse. Only 16% of the trade promotion events we studied were profitable, based on incremental sales of brands distributed through retailer warehouses. For many promotions, the cost of selling an incremental dollar of sales was *greater* than one dollar.

□ Judging from our aggregate statistics, managers have been spending too much of their marketing budgets on promotion (in lieu of advertising). Many companies could reduce their total advertising and promotion budgets *and* improve profitability.

To measure the productivity of television advertising, we use a technique known as a "split cable" market test. About 3,000 households in test markets receive ID cards that household members show when they purchase goods at scanner-equipped supermarkets. These supermarkets typically account for more than 90% of the total volume of all products sold in the area.

The test markets are far enough away from television stations that residents' only choice for good reception is cable TV. By agreement with the cable company and the advertiser, we intercept the cable signal before it reaches each household and send different advertisements to different households. To test advertising copy, some households receive advertisement A, while others simultaneously receive advertisement B. To test advertising weight, households receive different amounts of advertising for the same brand.

Split-cable tests typically run for one year, and we have conducted them for both new and established products. We control for variables such as past brand and category purchases and statistically adjust the sales data to account for the impact of promotions for the test brand or for competing brands. This instrumented test environment provides the ultimate degree of experimental control and is well suited for isolating the sales effect of advertising.

Some of the findings from our 360 split-cable tests conducted over the past decade support traditional assumptions. For example, most people believe that advertising is more effective for new brands than for established brands, and this turns out to be the case. We found that 59% of new-product advertising tests showed a positive impact on sales, compared with only 46% of the tests for established brands. Furthermore, when advertising showed a significant effect on a new product, the increase in sales averaged 21% across all new-product tests.

But in most respects, our findings clearly contradict conventional wisdom. In more than half of the established-brand experiments, increased advertising did not result in more sales.

Nor does advertising take a long time to work. When a particular advertising weight or copy is effective, it works relatively rapidly. Incremental sales begin to occur within six months. The converse of this finding is even more important. If advertising changes do not show an effect in six months, then they will not have any impact, even if continued for a year.

When advertising does boost sales, the extra profits often do not cover the increased media costs – at least in the short term. Company pay-out analyses are highly sensitive, and we have only partial pay-out statistics on a subset of our test database. They show that only about

Many companies could cut advertising and promotion budgets *and* improve profitability.

20% of advertising-weight tests pay out for established brands during the first year. For new products, profitable advertising ranges from 40% to 50%, reflecting the higher productivity of advertising spending on new products.

The Unprofitable Economics of Trade Promotions

	Cases	Gross Dollars
Baseline* (Sales that would have occurred during the four-week promotion period even without the promotion)	400	$ 4,000
Incremental Sales to Consumer† Due to one week of feature	100	$ 1,000
Due to 50% of stores with three weeks of display and price reduction	250	$ 2,500
Due to 50% of stores with four weeks of price reduction only	80	$ 800
Total	430	$ 4,300
Ten Weeks of Forward Buying by Retailers†	1,000	$10,000
Total Sales During Promotion	1,830	$18,300
Cost of Promotion ($18,300 x 15% Discount)		$ 2,745
Cost per Incremental Dollar of Sales (Promotion costs divided by total incremental sales)		$ .64
Promotion Efficiency (Incremental cases sold to consumer divided by total cases sold)		23.5%

*Assume weekly base sales of 100 cases and a list price of $10 per case.
†Based on our analysis of single-source data and retailer promotion purchases.

Despite the ideal conditions of this hypothetical example, the promotion ends up costing the manufacturer 64 cents for each incremental dollar it generates. Unless the product's gross margin is greater than 64%, the promotion will lose money.

However, the long-term effect of advertising is at least as substantial as its short-term effect. This is the upside to the downside that advertising works only about half the time. Even if increased advertising returns only half the money spent over the course of one year, it will break even on average if the long-term effects are taken into account.

We have evaluated the sales effect of advertising over the long term by analyzing 15 market tests up to two years after they ended. In these experiments, the test group viewed more advertisements than the control group during the test year. We then stopped the extra advertising and sent both groups the same amount. Across 15 cases, there was a demonstrable carryover effect. The sales increase for the groups receiving more advertising averaged 22% in the test year, 17% in the second year, and 6% in the third year. Although the carryover effect declined on average, in six cases it actually widened.

More important than the pattern is the magnitude of the carryover. On average, 76% of the difference observed in the test year persisted one year after the advertising increase was rolled back. Over a three-year period, the cumulative sales increase was at least twice the sales increase observed in the test year.

Why most promotions lose money

To evaluate trade promotions, we have developed computer programs that measure the marginal productivity of promotional events.[1] Anywhere from 30% to 90% of the time, a consumer product is not on promotion in a particular store. Using sales data from individual stores, the programs compare sales from these nonpromotion weeks with those from promotion weeks. Algorithms then project what the sales of the product would have been during the promotion week if the promotion had not taken place. This provides a baseline against which we can measure the incremental impact of the promotion. The only possible bias is that our programs may overestimate the incremental sales of a particular event since promotions tend to accelerate purchases by consumers. Thus we may mistakenly count purchases borrowed from a later period's normal sales as incremental sales caused by the promotion.

At first glance, our finding that only 16% of the promotions studied were profitable may seem surprising. But when you consider the economics underlying promotions, it is easy to see why. Consider the hypothetical example of a brand with very good support from retailers (see the exhibit "The Unprofitable Economics of Trade Promotions"). The brand promotes to the trade at a 15% price discount over a four-week period. Assume that all the stores in the market feature the brand for one week in their weekly newspaper advertising supplement. What's more, half the stores support the brand with three weeks of in-store display and consumer price reductions, while the other half only reduce the price but for the full four weeks. These are excellent trade-support statistics that would be hard to achieve in reality.

Nevertheless, when we compute the incremental sales generated from this excellent trade activity (also

1. For the technical details of these programs, see our "Promoter: An Automated Promotion Evaluation System," *Marketing Science*, Spring 1987, p. 101; and "Promotionscan: A System for Improving Promotion Productivity for Retailers and Manufacturers Using Scanner Store and Household Panel Data," Wharton School Marketing Department Working Paper (Philadelphia: University of Pennsylvania, February 1990).

assuming above-average consumer response), the promotion ends up costing 64 cents for each incremental dollar it generates. In other words, unless the product's gross margin is more than 64%, the promotion will lose money. The reason is that the manufacturer has to sell an extraordinarily high number of cases at the discounted price to cover the normal base sales that would have taken place without the promotion. What's more, the manufacturer must cover the practice of retailer "forward buying"—accumulating discounted inventory in the warehouse during the time window of the promotion and selling it later at the regular price. In fact, only about 23% of the cases sold on promotion are incremental in this example.

Forward buying helps explain why promotions often have a dramatic—and highly misleading—impact on a manufacturer's shipments. Typically, a retailer will take in thousands of cases during a promotion. But after a promotion, shipments will halt for several weeks while the retailer depletes its forward-buying inventory. Normally, that inventory has no benefit to the manufacturer. On the contrary, it substantially raises the costs of promotions and makes them unprofitable.

Another disadvantage of promotions is that unlike advertising, they almost never have a positive long-term effect on established brands. Promotions for new products may be quite productive because they encourage consumers to try an unfamiliar product. But the probability that consumers who buy an established brand on promotion will purchase it the next time is about the same as their likelihood of doing so even if no promotion had taken place. In fact, promotions for established brands usually attract either current users who would buy the product anyway or brand switchers who bounce between brands on deal.

Another hidden cost of promotions is competitive escalation. The advantage of running an extra promotion or offering higher incentives is usually short-lived. Competitors retaliate with promotions of their own, neutralizing whatever incre-

mental volume is generated. The most insidious escalation is that of trade promotion discounts. When retailers are offered higher discounts once, they come to expect them regularly.

The flip side is de-escalation—a cycle where competitors refrain from undercutting each other's profits through promotions. Discontinuing a money-losing promotion not only stops a manufacturer's losses; it also sends a de-escalation signal, which, if heeded by competitors (and chances are higher if the manufacturer's brand is a market leader), ends up improving profits even more. However, if de-escalation doesn't take place, then cutting promotions will cost sales and market share even as it increases profits. Only if de-escalation works can profits be enhanced without losing sales or share.

Fact-based strategies and tactics

With single-source data, managers can balance investments in advertising and promotion to improve the contribution of each to long-term profit. Intelligent use of the data can help the ad manager determine not only when and where to increase spending but also when and where to decrease it.

The idea is to start with a zero budget and allocate money incrementally to various advertising and promotion options. The goal is to identify the option that marginally contributes most to the long-term profitability of the product. Allocations should continue on this incremental basis until all options that provide a suitable return on the incremental investment are found.

Since advertising doesn't always work, the first challenge is to maximize the chances of getting productive campaigns. Ad execs should increase spending as long as a particular campaign remains productive and cut back as soon as market tests show its productivity declining significantly. Meanwhile, they should constantly search for new, more compelling advertising and test it against the old.

For new products, advertising can provide significant help when it ful-

fills its primary role of communicating product news. Increasing weight behind effective new-product advertising is a productive strategy. Because new-product advertising primarily influences trial, which may lead to repeat purchases, its effectiveness is likely to be long term. The combination of a successful new product and successful advertising is rare. When this happens, it is no time for skimping.

To determine whether a particular new-product advertisement is working, test it at different weight levels in test markets before the national rollout. If the new product sells as well in those groups with low exposure as in those with high exposure, then heavy spending is not necessary. Conversely, if the higher weight groups try the product faster or more frequently, then higher levels of advertising make sense—if the company considers the long-term value of the new triers greater than the advertising cost. Thus testing "How high is up?" is an important tactic for new products.

Once new-product advertising has generated trials and positioned the new product in the market, continuing with the same large advertising budgets may not be necessary. In fact, without compelling new copy, approximately one-half of established-

> **Use single-source test sites as "lead markets" for national advertising campaigns.**

brand advertising does not produce any incremental sales. On the other hand, fresh copy for established products can prove extremely productive. Positive advertising effects on sales will continue long after the advertising has stopped, generally for at least one year.

These findings imply a very different form of "pulsing" for many established products. Current practice

Customizing Promotions for Local Markets

	Retailer Support (Weighted weeks product is on promotion)	Consumer Response (Incremental sales per week of features and displays)	Unsupported Price Reductions (Weeks of price reductions with no features or displays)
Local Market			
Seattle	106	117	156

Recommended Action
Better support of price reductions should contribute to the higher-than-average consumer response.

Houston	120	115	85

High retailer support and customer response combined with low unsupported price reductions mean that the manufacturer should continue doing what it's doing.

Tampa	116	60	89

Retailers are supporting the product well, but consumers aren't responding.
It's time to improve the quality of features and displays.

Boston	82	115	102

Retailer support is below average, but consumers are still responding well.
More features and displays could build on an already good situation.

Philadelphia	99	156	132

Consumer response is very high, but so is the number of unsupported price reductions.
Supporting reductions with features and displays should increase sales and profits.

Kansas City	79	72	72

Both retailer support and consumer response are below national levels.
It's time for more frequent and higher quality features and displays.

The numbers index promotion activity and consumer response in local markets to the national average (= 100) and suggest ways to improve future promotions in each market.

is to pulse in short bursts of two to four weeks, on and off, using the same advertising each time. We would recommend pulses of at least six months, carried out over several years and using different advertising campaigns.

When advertising cannot demonstrate that it is incrementally contributing to sales of an established product (as shown by tests comparing the current advertising level with lower budgets), cut it back to some lower maintenance level – perhaps even to zero. Do not increase spending until a new campaign has demonstrated greater productivity. It is possible to estimate the likely incremental effect of a new campaign by showing both the old campaign at the old weight and the new campaign at several different weights to matched groups in test markets.

Having identified an effective new campaign, a company should run it at a high level nationally until it no longer shows any incremental sales effect, measured by comparing it with no advertising in a test market. As soon as this new campaign's incremental sales effect stops, the advertiser should cut it back until yet another effective campaign can be developed.

Because of the risk associated with radical decreases in advertising, an even safer approach is to use the single-source test markets as "lead markets" for national advertising. For example, conduct a six- to nine-month test comparing a lower advertising weight with the current national weight. If the lower weight does not harm sales in the test markets, implement it nationally. In the test markets, however, continue sending the "normal" weight advertising to the group that has been receiving it. That way, if sales to the test households exposed to the lower advertising weight begin to decline compared with sales to normal-

weight households, the national advertising budget can be immediately returned to the higher levels.

This strategy gives the decision maker a cushion so that decreasing national advertising poses little risk. Should the original decision prove to be a mistake, the company can return the national campaign to normal levels some six to nine months before sales begin to decline. Of course, a continuous search for new and more effective campaigns should occur simultaneously with this lower advertising.

Companies can use similar techniques to identify productive promotions. In promotions as in advertising, there is a premium on ingenuity and creativity. An effective promotion idea can be three or four times as efficient as the typical prior promotion. A company should spend significant resources to develop creative, hard-to-imitate promotion events, then use single-source data to

Identifying Mutually Beneficial Promotions

	Jewel XYZ Promotion Event	XYZ Event Plus One More Week of Feature and Display
Incremental Cases Sold to Consumer	933	1,633
Nonpromoted Retail Case Price	$90	$90
Gross Incremental Dollars	$83,970	$149,670
Retailer Price Reduction	16%	16%
Cost of Retailer Price Reduction	$13,435	$23,947
Promoted Wholesale Case Price	$50	$50
Cost of Goods to Retailer	$46,650	$83,150
Retailer Profit	$23,885	$42,573

By comparing the results of the XYZ event with single-source data from other promotions in the same market, we determined that with only one more week of feature and display, Jewel would have increased its profit by $18,688, and the manufacturer would have sold an extra 700 cases.

test the idea. Not all ideas will make it past the test, but those that do will enhance profits. And depending on diminishing returns and competitive response, a company may be able to use the new event or idea more than once, helping further to amortize the investment in promotion development.

Finally, marketing managers can also apply the same analytical concepts to promotion and advertising decisions for particular local areas and for a manufacturer's key accounts—if they use the single-source data carefully. For example, the data can provide market-by-market estimates of promotional response and retailer support that may offer insights for allocating promotion funds and making necessary tactical changes.

The exhibit "Customizing Promotions for Local Markets" divides geographic markets according to their levels of promotion response and trade-promotion support for a particular product, then summarizes suggested actions. We index each market to national averages for the number of weeks (weighted by store volume) that the brand was on some type of promotion, as well as by the markets' average response (incremental sales per week of feature or display activity) and the

weeks the brand was on price reduction only and not supported by feature or display ("unsupported price reductions").

The decision rules that support the actions are only a somewhat crude way to point management in a generally more profitable direction. Those markets with above-average unsupported price reductions might need greater featuring and display support from the retailer. Those low in promotion response probably require higher quality promotions—larger newspaper features, say, or better display locations.

Similarly, companies can use single-source data to target key accounts and isolate mutually beneficial situations for the retailer and the manufacturer. The exhibit "Identifying Mutually Beneficial Markets" shows how Jewel Food Stores could have almost doubled its profits from a particular promotion event (here called the XYZ event) by adding one more week of feature and display. The result would be good for the manufacturer as well because incremental cases sold would have increased from 933 to 1,633 without any additional investment.

A new role for the sales force

One final caveat about these new marketing strategies merits discuss-

ing. Single-source data measure the effect of advertising and promotions on consumers, *not* on the distribution of a given product by retailers. One of the traditional uses of both advertising and promotion has been to convince retailers that the manufacturer supports the product and that the brand will pull consumers into the stores. Thus if a company cuts back on unproductive advertising between pulses or discontinues ineffective promotions, it runs the risk that retailers will interpret the move as a lack of support and therefore cut back on distribution.

To avoid this predicament, the sales force has a new and extremely important job to do. It must communicate to retailers that unproductive advertising with no consumer pull has no value to the retailer or the manufacturer. Likewise, smart retailers will begin demanding hard evidence on the consumer pull of advertising instead of merely being impressed with large media budgets.

The role of the sales force in promotion also will change. Instead of viewing trade promotions as a competitive payment to make sure the brand has distribution, sales personnel have to demonstrate to retailers how specific promotions will increase their incremental profits.

Taking advantage of this opportunity will require salespeople to have greater analytical abilities than they have needed in the past. In effect, they will have to become marketers in partnership with retailers. The retailers, like the manufacturers, now know what items are moving because they are seeing the same single-source data. As more retailers become sophisticated users of this information, it will be more difficult for manufacturers to get them to execute promotion programs that are not in retailers' best interests. Over time, there will be a bigger and bigger productivity difference between simply giving a retailer a price discount and hoping for the best and giving a price discount to support a well-documented, mutually beneficial promotion program.

*In terms of share of voice,
some companies are "profit takers" and
others, "investors."*

Ad Spending: Maintaining Market Share

by John Philip Jones

Why do sales volume and brand advertising budgets move in lockstep? Most manufacturers use the case rate system, or one of its many variants, which ties a brand's ad budget to its sales by allocating a certain number of advertising cents or dollars to each case sold. This practice is seldom challenged, but it raises three tough questions:

1. *Does this system tell the advertiser whether the brand's budget is the right sum for generating optimum sales and maximum profit?* The answer to this question must be "no." This is because the procedure is directed inward to the brand's costs, not outward to the market, where the brand's sales are determined.

2. *Do advertisers fully appreciate the close link between the advertising budget of a brand and the profit it earns?* Advertisers normally confine their thinking to the long-term benefits to income of the extra sales that advertising generates. But there is also a short-term effect. Since advertising is a residual expense, any addition to the budget comes straight out of profit. (And a cut enhances profit—hence the prevalence of fourth quarter ad cancellations to compensate for the profit lost by shortfalls in sales.)

Moreover, advertising can have a geared effect on profit if the brand's net earnings ratio is smaller than its advertising to sales ratio. A rise or drop in advertising will then exert a greater proportional effect on profit.

3. *What can advertisers do other than overspend or underspend?* Until better budgetary methods are developed, believed in, and used, the answer to this question is "nothing."

Think of the impact that marginal productivity improvement would have—especially for major advertisers who, without blinking an eye, spend tens of millions of dollars above the line on campaigns for each of many brands.

What all this amounts to is an enormous need for more efficient advertising budgeting, and the way to get it is through better tools to help advertisers and agencies. But to be of practical use to those who manage brands, such tools must be simple in all respects. There must be no confusion about how they are constructed or how they can be employed to tackle specific situations. And they must also amount to more than theoretical constructs; they must be recognizably derived from the experience of brands in the real world. There is no shortage of black boxes, but we cannot discern, comprehend, or accept the contents of the majority of them.

Penetration supercharge

This article describes a simple empirical tool to help determine a brand's advertising budget. It emerged from an examination of large and small brands, a piece of work undertaken to throw light on a hypothesis that large brands are less advertising intensive than small brands—that is, per dollar of sales value, less advertising is spent on larger brands than on smaller ones. To express this point another way, a given number of dollars spent on large brands produces more sales than a similar number spent on small brands.

I carried out the investigation in cooperation with J. Walter Thomp-

John Philip Jones is professor and chairman of the advertising department at the Newhouse School of Public Communications, Syracuse University. From 1953 until 1980, he worked in the advertising agency field, chiefly with J. Walter Thompson in London and elsewhere in Europe. He has written What's in a Name? Advertising & the Concept of Brands *and* Does It Pay to Advertise? *(Lexington Books, 1986 and 1989).*

son. In the fall of 1987, the ad agency's headquarters sent its offices around the world a questionnaire seeking a limited amount of clearly defined and solidly based factual data. Some 242 completed questionnaires came back to New York from 23 countries, each referring to a single product category in a single country. The data covered 1,096 advertised brands.

Most of the brands covered were repeat-purchase packaged goods well-known to consumers and carrying substantial producer names like Kellogg, Unilever, and Procter & Gamble. The markets for such goods are almost invariably oligopolistic. They also tend to be stationary: in developed countries, I estimate, 90% of the sales of all brands of packaged goods are made in markets that show very little growth beyond that associated with a gradually increasing population. Sales and advertising expenditures of individual brands tend to remain stable, and their advertising to sales ratios normally range from 4% to 8%.

The best way to examine advertising intensity is to gauge the advertising to sales ratio on a brand-by-brand basis. This requires reliable estimates both of the brand's advertising expenditure and its sales value. While the former figure is easy to arrive at, a tight estimate of sales on the basis of the retail audit or consumer panel data is virtually impossible to make. It is necessary to find another way to evaluate the importance of advertising in relation to sales.

Fortunately, there is another way to calculate advertising intensity: comparison of a brand's share of market, on a volume or value basis, with its share of voice (the brand's share of the total value of the main media exposure in the product category).

The rationale for this method of calculating advertising intensity is that the cost structure of one brand in a market tends to be similar to that of any other. Moreover, the producers of rival brands keep track of one another's advertising expenditures (a characteristic of oligopolistic competition). As a result, makers of brands of a similar volume tend to spend similar amounts on advertis-

ing, and a brand that is twice the size of another tends to receive twice as much advertising expenditure.

This situation gives rise to the concept of a normal approximate similarity between a brand's share of market and its share of voice. There are obviously some erratic exceptions, and nothing can be done to allow for these. But there are also consistent exceptions relating to brands of different sizes.

In examining these consistent exceptions, I put the data into two categories (share of market is on a volume basis):

1. Profit-taking brands, or underspenders – those whose share of voice is the same as or below their share of market.

2. Investment brands, or overspenders – those whose share of voice is clearly above their share of market.

The fact that in every market some brands are unadvertised means that the average share of voice – shared among fewer brands – is for mathematical reasons above the average share of market – shared among more brands. So it is not quite true to say that the normal and stable relationship for an advertised brand is a parity of share of market and share of voice; rather, it is a share of market and a *higher* share of voice. In markets where there are important but

unadvertised store brands, the difference can be quite large. But in all circumstances, if a brand spends the same share of voice as its share of market, it is (at least slightly) underspending.

In the table "Profit Taking and Investment Brands," the brands in these two categories have been collected in groups covering 3 percentage points of market share. (A sample based on single percentage points of share would not have been reliable.) Among those brands with small market shares, profit takers are in a minority. But the proportion of profit takers consistently grows as the brands get more powerful; of those with a share of 16% or more, nearly three out of five have a proportionately smaller share of voice.

The picture is remarkably clear, and there are three forces at work that are responsible for it.

The first is the heavy advertising infusions, exceeding their market share percentages, given to new, burgeoning brands (which are, of course, nearly always small). Indeed, A.C. Nielsen, on the basis of its extensive knowledge of the fortunes of new brands, has long recommended this budget strategy. This factor accounts for the high shares of voice of many small-share brands. One of the causes of smaller brands' lower profitability, compared with larger

Profit-Taking and Investment Brands

	All Brands	Percentage of Profit-Taking Brands (share of voice equal to or smaller than share of market)	Percentage of Investment Brands (share of voice larger than share of market)
Total Market Share	1,096	44%	56%
1% to 3%	224	27	73
4% to 6%	218	37	63
7% to 9%	153	41	59
10% to 12%	112	45	55
13% to 15%	77	56	44
16% and over	312	59	41

Profile of Brands with 13% Market Share or More

	Percentage of All Brands	Percentage of Profit-Taking Brands	Percentage of Investment Brands
Brands with: Slightly Rising Share	43%	39%	49%
Static Share	26	28	24
Slightly Falling Share	31	33	27
Premium Price	32	28	37
Average Price	51	54	46
Below Average Price	17	18	17

Sample Size: 389 (226 profit-taking brands and 163 investment brands)

brands, is the trade-off between advertising and profit—more advertising, less profit.

The second factor is the all-too-common practice of milking older and often quite large brands. This is a tempting strategy for manufacturers because of the short-term effect in increasing a brand's earnings of a sharp reduction in advertising and promotional support. A belief in brand life-cycle theory sometimes persuades manufacturers to adopt this strategy. The strategy is self-fulfilling because the very act of cutting support when a brand's sales are turning down, in the expectation that a downturn is inevitable, will accelerate the downturn. An examination of the 389 most potent brands in the sample (see the second table on brands with at least 13% market share) shows that a third of the profit takers are on a slightly falling sales trend, which suggests that many if not most of these are being milked.

The third factor is an advertising economy of scale. Many large brands flourish with shares of voice consistently below their shares of market. Two-thirds of the profit takers in the second table, for instance, are holding or improving their market shares. For such brands, advertising works harder, dollar for dollar, than it does for most smaller brands—a clear

economy of scale. This is one of the great strengths of the branding phenomenon. Another is illustrated in the same table: 28% of the profit-taking brands command premium prices in the market.

The cause and operating mechanisms of this scale economy are not known with certainty, but they are thought to relate to a characteristic of consumer purchasing behavior: a tendency for popular brands to benefit from above-average purchase and repurchase frequency. I call this phenomenon penetration supercharge.

Average share of voice

The table "Average Share of Voice Compared with Share of Market" concentrates on typical packaged goods markets that are balanced competitively and thus yield data with the maximum internal consistency. For each brand I calculated the difference between share of voice and share of market and averaged these differences within each family of brands. As before, the picture is fairly consistent. Brands in the 1% to 3% range overinvest in advertising by an average of 5 percentage points, and brands in the 28% to 30% range underinvest by an average of 5 percentage points. The size brackets between follow an approximate continuum.

These data can be set out diagrammatically (see the curve comparing SOV with SOM). By interpolating a brand's market share into the curve, a marketer can ascertain the share of voice for all brands of that size. This figure can be converted without much trouble into an advertising expenditure number, providing a normal expenditure level against which the brand's actual expenditure can be measured.

By breaking out the packaged goods brands with market shares of

Average Share of Voice Compared with Share of Market

Share of Market	Share of Voice Above or Below Share of Market (percentage points)
1% to 3%	+5
4% to 6%	+4
7% to 9%	+2
10% to 12%	+4
13% to 15%	+1
16% to 18%	+2
19% to 21%	No Difference
22% to 24%	−3
25% to 27%	−5
28% to 30%	−5

Sample Size: 666 brands in 117 markets
(Of total samples, markets with at least four advertised brands and free of domination by a single brand.)

Curve Comparing Share of Voice with Share of Market

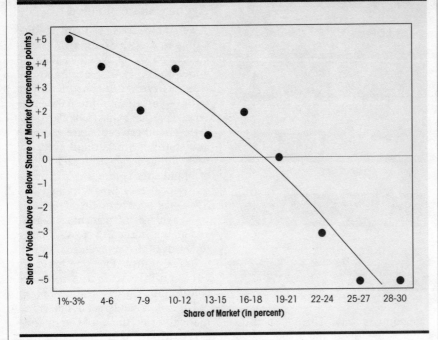

fers a change of viewpoint, a shift from the usual inward-directed system, based on the brand's case rate, outward to the market. This viewpoint is useful in weighing facts from different sources, such as:

□ *Average share of voice.* The particular value of this measure is in helping determine the level of underinvestment that may be acceptable for larger brands, subject to area testing.

□ *Marketplace trends.* As I have mentioned, most packaged goods markets are stationary. The value of studying stationary markets is to determine normal levels of the main marketing variables, including budgets. But the existence of normal levels does not imply stasis; gradual changes are always possible and often take place in the long term.

□ *The brand's response to advertising pressure.* Many long-established brands have built a useful track record of experience with varying levels of advertising pressure. In many cases, econometric studies have produced a specific advertising elasticity – an estimate of the marginal sales increase that follows a 1% boost in the ad pressure put behind the brand. Marketplace testing of different levels of such pressure to determine the coefficients, now a rare procedure, is bound to increase in importance. It should be on the agenda of all major advertisers.

□ *The brand's cost structure.* If the first three factors add up to a higher expenditure than this one does, the advertiser obviously is in a difficult position. The company must rethink its short-term profit target for the brand and decide whether acceptance of a reduced (or zero or negative) profit makes sense for a while in the hope that the brand will pay out and

---

13% or more according to their market share trends, I came up with the findings shown in the last table. The average very popular brand with a rising sales trend is profit taking. But there are signs that greater underinvestment imperils sales, and if the underinvestment opens out to 4 percentage points for the average brand, sales will turn into a decline. Naturally, individual brands vary. In particular, weaker brands can be expected to stand less underinvestment, and stronger brands rather more underinvestment.

One of the strongest brands extant is Lux. Unilever's toilet soap has occupied a major share of its category for more than 60 years, and in many countries it has reached extraordinary levels of consumer penetration and purchase frequency. It boasts an aggregate volume brand share in 30 countries of 17% and an overall share of voice of 14%. Powered by this level of advertising, Lux is holding its market share and on occasion marginally adding to it. Evidence from areas where Lux's advertising has been cut back indicates that a drop in share of voice to less than 12% will produce a loss in market share. The threshold level of underinvestment for this

brand is therefore 5 percentage points below its market share.

The data demonstrate, I must emphasize, that profit taking by planned underinvestment in advertising is a normal (and successful) policy only for popular brands. The others – those with a market share under 13% – are on average in an investment situation, with a higher share of voice than share of market.

A budgetary planning tool

The device I have described has two important features. First, it supplies a measure, a useful objective comparison between one brand's advertising expenditure in its marketplace and the expenditures of many other brands of a comparable size in different marketplaces. Second, it of-

---

Breakdown of Brands with Market Shares of at Least 13%

	Share of Voice *Below* Share of Market (percentage points)
Brands with Rising Trends (83)	–1
Brands with Static Trends (53)	–3
Brands with Declining Trends (64)	–4

recoup the investment by a certain date. This is a worst case scenario, but it is a more attractive option than spending what the brand can afford in the likelihood that the amount will be too little to be effective.

It is possible, however, that the first three factors will lead to a smaller expenditure than the fourth. In this case, there is a good reason now to conduct some carefully evaluated area testing of advertising down-weighting. Anything more than a marginal loss of sales experienced as a result may endanger the brand's "critical mass," with its ability to generate scale economies. But this outcome is by no means certain. If competitive brands also reduce the budget, the outcome will probably be no loss of aggregate sales in the market and reasonable stability in the shares of the individual brands. Even if the brand goes it alone, sales may not suffer markedly.

Some advertisers might fear that an advertising cutback on their part would arouse competitors to implement an opportunistic advertising increase. But the consequences of such an increase need not be feared unduly for two reasons:

1. The advertising elasticity of most brands is low, which promises a very limited sales uplift in response to an increase in advertising pressure.

2. The profitability of the extra advertising pressure—measured by the difference (if any) between the income from the marginal increase in earnings from the higher sales and the cost of the extra advertising—is even less likely.

It has been estimated that as many as 95% of tests of stepped-up advertising pressure are failures.[1] It would be very surprising indeed if this were also true of tests of *reduced* advertising pressure. In these, the very lack of responsiveness of sales to changes in advertising pressure operates in the advertiser's favor. A small sales loss means a small profit loss, making it likely that the advertising saving will exceed this amount.

1. Callaghan OHerlihy, "How to Test the Sales Effects of Advertising," *Admap*, January 1980, p.32.

Reprint 90108

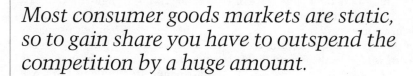

Most consumer goods markets are static, so to gain share you have to outspend the competition by a huge amount.

Ad Spending: Growing Market Share

by James C. Schroer

Remember Schlitz? Electrasol? Bosco? Ipana? Remember the days when brand loyalty grew year by year? Today's most successful brands of consumer goods were built by heavy advertising and marketing investments long ago. But recently, many marketers have lost sight of the connection between advertising spending and market share. They practice the art of discounting: cutting ad budgets to fund price promotions or fatten quarterly earnings. They may win the volume battle today, but they lose the competitive war.

The marketers at some companies, however, remember that brand value and consumer preference for brands drive market share. They also know that price promotion buys shelf position. Most important, they understand the balance of advertising and promotion expenditures needed to build brands and gain share, market by market, regardless of growth trends in the product categories where they compete.

Procter & Gamble, for example, has built its Jif and Folger's brands from single-digit shares to category leaders. In peanut butter and coffee, P&G invests more in advertising and less in discounting than its major competitors. Kellogg and General

> ▌ In most markets, big competitors are in a stalemate.

Mills, waging an escalating ad spending war in breakfast cereals, together now command 65% of the market—and their stock trades at much higher valuations than other food companies. Coke and Pepsi invest so much in advertising that they make it cost prohibitive for anyone else to compete with them. Together they own 70% of the market.

What do these great marketers have in common? Among other things, awareness of a key factor in advertising: consistent investment spending. They do not raid their budgets to ratchet earnings up for a few quarters. They know that advertising should not be managed as a discretionary variable cost.

The advertising weapon

Let's examine the impact of advertising spending in situations where competitors' products are more or less the same (for example, people can't really tell one paper towel or deodorant from another), and competitors' marketing, promotion, and advertising people appear to be equally effective. Of course, truly superior or inferior advertising *content* is an important factor in the gain or loss of market share, but I am not talking about that here.

Under such circumstances, the following patterns emerge:

☐ Advertising spending can determine advances and retreats in market share—but only when a big spending difference among competitors has been maintained for a long time. Judging from studies of many consumer products over the past several years, this difference must be at least double the main rival's outlay. The relationship between spending and share change appears after about 18 months, and reliable correlations can be established after 3 years.

☐ Most of the time, competitors are in a state of equilibrium where the leaders' market shares remain stable despite marginal changes in their ad expenditures. Competitors that understand the spending game will establish this equilibrium at a level so high that no upstart can afford the extra sustained investment needed to increase its share.

☐ A competitor with an aggressive ad spending strategy will keep up the

James C. Schroer, a vice president of Booz, Allen & Hamilton, focuses on marketing strategy for the consulting firm's consumer goods clients. He spent eight years as a marketing executive, first for STP Corporation and then for the Wagner Division of McGraw-Edison.

attack only so long as it is adding to market share. By pouring in enough dollars to convince this aggressor that the market has returned to stalemate, the combatants can force a return to share equilibrium levels.

☐ Therefore, unsupportable, unprofitable levels of ad spending will not continue indefinitely.

☐ Ad spending requirements powerfully contribute to industry consolidation. Because the equilibrium point is likely to be high, in most cases no more than two or three players can generate the volume needed to maintain the necessary amount of advertising expenditure.

☐ These relationships exist on an individual market basis, not on a national level. Indeed, who would expect an advertising push in New York City to drive share movements in Seattle? In fact, the cases in which I have observed share upheavals have been those where the loser was focusing on ad budgets at the national level and was blind, or did not react, to a rival's attacks with large spending differentials in particular markets.

Ad spending and market share

These observations will become clearer with reference to the two charts relating ad spending to market share in consumer packaged goods industries. The first chart shows competitive equilibrium, in which the largest and smallest players each enjoy a share of market (SOM) somewhat bigger than their share of ad spending (SOV). The midsize competitor (#2) is laying out disproportionately more on advertising than its share of market. In this situation, all players' market shares tend to remain static. It is very difficult to force shifts in share through ad spending.

Conventional analysis suggests that the market leader's SOV can be less than its SOM. I agree. The leader enjoys a scale advantage enabling it to outspend the followers at a lower per-unit cost.

Conventional wisdom also suggests that smaller players overspend, taking a share of voice greater than share of market. I disagree. This logic leads to a spending war that the smaller players cannot hope to win.

A smaller competitor trying to exploit a differentiated niche should not try to grow beyond narrow limits. It would be folly to launch an ad offensive on the leaders.

But the midsize player, to maintain an SOV close to the leader, is forced to outspend #1 (in relation to its market share). Going for a large piece of the market, this competitor cannot hide in a niche.

In this state of equilibrium, company #2 is likely to be less profitable

It's folly for a niche player to launch an ad offensive against the leaders.

than company #1 because the latter can maintain a competitive voice level even while spending less than its "fair share." Of course, a small player that is content in a niche can be very profitable too as long as it maintains a differentiated position.

The equilibrium pattern suggests the difficulty of sustaining an intermediate position – which helps explain why, in many categories, consolidation has reduced the number to only two or three dominant brands. Coke and Pepsi in colas, Folger's and Maxwell House in coffee, Bartles & Jaymes and Seagram's in wine coolers. But of course there are often very healthy regional competitors in market segments.

Coors, an extremely profitable niche brand in its early years, despite a negligible share of voice, has found the going tough on a national scale. The "Rocky Mountain Beer" once enjoyed such a mystique that people drove or flew literally thousands of miles to procure a case. Then, deciding to take on Anheuser-Busch and Miller nationally, Coors fell victim to the conventional wisdom, spending SOV>SOM.

Coors can't afford to compete as a mass brand. Despite annual ad spending of $80 million or so, Coors remains dwarfed by Miller at more than $200 million and Bud at more

than $300 million. Coors Premium's volume has declined despite a national rollout. Not surprisingly, Coors's advertising recently has shifted back to its Rocky Mountain niche positioning from its "Coors is the One" mass positioning. (Last September, signaling a new determination to challenge the leaders, Coors announced it was buying most of Stroh's assets. While this makes Coors a larger company, it does not help Coors Premium beer solve its ad expenditure problems with A-B and Miller.)

Market leaders win the ad spending war for market share by creating or exploiting *dis*equilibrium and outspending their competitors by a wide margin for a sustained period. They use ad spending as a competitive weapon, and they benefit from a relative share of voice effect on market share.

If the two leaders have SOVs that stay within about 10 percentage points of each other, then competitive equilibrium exists. If, however, one rival's share of voice gets an infusion and eventually exceeds the other's by 20 to 30 percentage points, then share changes may well take place that can be correlated to ad spending. The second chart shows the dynamic.

You may ask, "What company would be foolish enough to let a competitor outspend it by more than double?" The answer is, many companies. They either can't or don't spend enough in each market. Given the downward pressure on advertising budgets created by the need to hype earnings to avoid a buyout, or to pay interest on debt after the buyout – plus the tendency of marketers to shift ad dollars into promotion dollars to buy shelf space for increasingly complex product lines from increasingly powerful retailers – underspending situations are not hard to find.

They are particularly easy to find on a market-by-market basis. Even a company whose national investment in advertising is adequate is often vulnerable to attack in markets where its spending falls below the level needed to maintain equilibrium. Very few companies determine

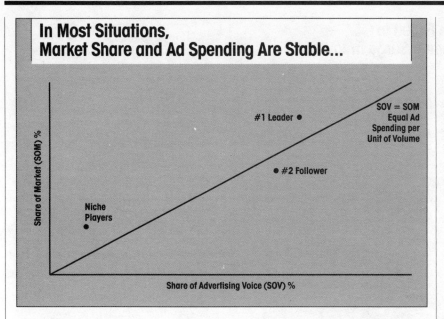

In Most Situations, Market Share and Ad Spending Are Stable...

advertising budgets on the basis of share of voice by market. Instead, they determine their ad budgets on a national basis.

Then they divert some of the budget to "heavy-up" their ad spending in markets where their brands are not doing well. This is not only wrong for the reasons I have mentioned—in these low-share markets the odds of winning the spending campaign against the leaders are poor—but it also leaves the companies' most important (higher share) markets vulnerable to assault by a competitor that understands how to use the relative share of voice effect to its advantage. This makes the marketer very vulnerable to challenges in markets where share of voice falls disproportionately low.

Relative share of voice effects largely explain Anheuser-Busch's remarkable share gains. In Iowa in the early 1980s, the popularly priced and often price-promoted brands Pabst and Old Milwaukee held leading positions. But they invited attack by spending less than equilibrium levels. A-B entered this segment with its Busch brand, but the leaders chose not to defend their positions with extra advertising (see the chart "Pabst and Old Milwaukee Failed to Respond..."). A-B outspent them by a wide margin, though not by much in absolute terms, attaining a relative share of voice exceeding 2 (twice as much as the target competitor). In

the 1984 to 1986 period, Busch grew at rates exceeding 30%; today the brand is challenging for popular segment leadership in Iowa. For Pabst or Old Milwaukee to counterattack now would be prohibitively expensive.

In this type of disequilibrium situation, share growth is a quantifiable function of ad spending. This can be confirmed through regression analy-

sis. For a variety of products, analysis has revealed, a share of voice "premium" equivalent to 20 to 30 percentage points of total category advertising spending was necessary to generate share gains that could be correlated with ad spending increases. (Private-label spending was excluded.) Correlation coefficients reached a maximum of about 0.5—not bad for a single independent variable in a situation in which multiple influences were clearly at work.

Such gains do not come cheap. A 25-point premium may imply spending twice as much as your competitor. Hence my conviction that relative share of voice needs to be roughly 2 to make the spending effect observable.

These dynamics, it's important to note, are always expressed in share of total category or segment spending, not in absolute terms. This assumes that total spending is enough to drive primary demand and each competitor can influence only its own share. If total category ad spending falls below a certain threshold, these assumptions will not hold because any competitor would be in a position to

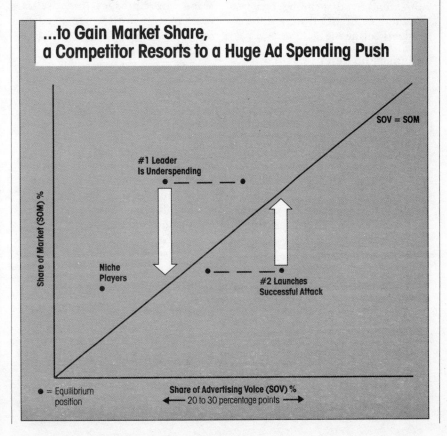

...to Gain Market Share, a Competitor Resorts to a Huge Ad Spending Push

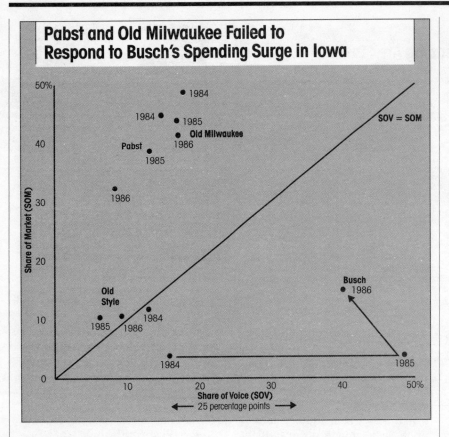

Pabst and Old Milwaukee Failed to Respond to Busch's Spending Surge in Iowa

stimulate primary demand. For this reason, the relative SOV logic does not extend to ad spending for new products or highly differentiated products occupying niches.

Offense and defense

Rational competitors halt their ad offensives when they cease to produce share gains and equilibrium reigns once again. The implication for defense is clear: spend to deter attack. Assailants must recognize the signs and be prepared to back off.

Anheuser-Busch apparently competes with these points in mind, despite its reputation for pouring money into advertising. When rivals seem likely to defend themselves aggressively, A-B keeps its ad spending close to the equilibrium levels. In the Los Angeles light beer market, for instance, Anheuser has withheld a heavy assault against Miller Lite, the leader—unlike its behavior elsewhere to promote Bud Light.

Anheuser's restraint in Los Angeles makes sense. If it struck at

1. See, for example, John Philip Jones, *What's in a Name?* (Lexington, Mass.: Lexington Books, 1986), chapter 8.

Miller Lite, Miller would probably retaliate dollar for dollar, and neither brand would prosper. Anheuser is wiser to sally forth where an effective defense is less likely and the cost of success lower, as in Iowa.

Much has been written about the so-called advertising response function.[1] There is some agreement that the productivity of ad dollars rises as budgets grow from zero to a meaningful level, and then the law of diminishing returns sets in. Piling on more dollars becomes less and less productive. Hence you get an S-shaped function by plotting sales against ad expenditures, as the fourth chart demonstrates.

My associates and I have been unable to confirm a correlation between sales volume and the advertising budget, and that is what led us to look for the relative share of voice effect. The principle says: If I yell loud and you yell loud, the audience will hear both of us. But if I start yelling louder when you are quieter, the audience will hear only me.

Market leaders have this problem. Spending at levels loud enough to be heard, they are in a zero-sum joust-

ing match. For either company #1 or company #2, cutting share of voice too much can be a disaster. The share of voice effect takes hold, and the "quieter" competitor loses share while the "louder" competitor gains. Similarly, an obvious run at an SOV advantage is likely to spark an unprofitable war as both players spend to maintain equilibrium.

The shrewd marketer, therefore, picks its attacks carefully, targeting markets wisely, aiming at markets for share gain where the competitor is vulnerable, markets where that competitor is (perhaps knowingly) underspending, markets where a voice can be raised without breaking the budget.

The niche player's concern has to be spending enough to be heard at all by its target audience. RC Cola, avoiding Coke and Pepsi's $200 million battle for the mass-market, young soft drink consumer, has targeted a smaller segment, the adult soft drink market. Historically, RC's comparatively meager $10 million ad budget appeared sufficient to hold RC's niche. RC's recently announced ad spending increase to $20 million is a drop in the bucket; like Coors, RC cannot delude itself into entering a war with the leaders. RC should not think share of voice; rather, it should spend the minimum necessary to have adequate reach and frequency, and not much more.

SOV and marketing strategy

These observations on the relationship between share of ad spend-

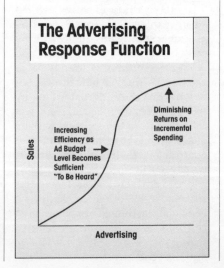

The Advertising Response Function

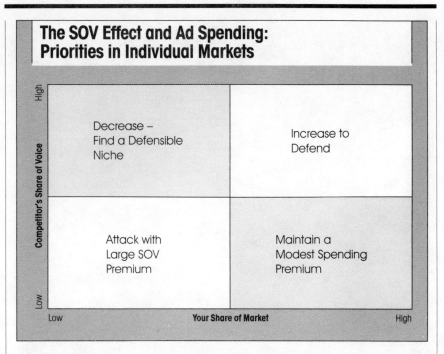

The SOV Effect and Ad Spending: Priorities in Individual Markets

	Low ← **Your Share of Market** → High
High (Competitor's Share of Voice)	Decrease – Find a Defensible Niche	Increase to Defend
Low	Attack with Large SOV Premium	Maintain a Modest Spending Premium

ing and market share may encourage marketers to rethink their spending policies and geographic priorities along four dimensions:

1. A national approach to marketing may get you in trouble. Instead of applying the same formula everywhere, marketing managers are wise to choose a strategy, and the tools to be used, for particular markets at particular times. This often requires a different set of ad expenditure priorities than consumer goods companies normally adopt. The chart "The SOV Effect and Ad Spending" shows the recommended priorities.

Rather than challenge competitors in markets where it is weak and they are the leaders, as is commonly the case, the company does best by picking its shots and targeting markets where competitors are underspending. In those, the upstart will spend at a significant share of voice premium to try to grow share. Merely matching the competition's spending in those markets is unlikely to do the attacker much good, unless its objective is only to hold its position. (Naturally, the company's own high-share markets must at the same time be defended at all costs. Otherwise, it ends up like Pabst in Iowa.)

2. Marketing managers must understand competitors' relative cost positions. Without a systematic cost advantage, it is unlikely that the spending premium needed to gain share can be sustained very long. But with a cost advantage, the attacker can continue the offensive a long time. P&G is perhaps the best at creating a systematic cost advantage and then using the savings for ad spending to sustain ad wars that frustrate the competition – as P&G inexorably gains share.

3. Marketers have to resist the lure of short-term profits. Almost any brand can survive ad budget cuts for months or even years, and that resilience tempts the marketer to maximize near-term earnings. But think how Electrasol, Ipana, and others scrimped on marketing and product investments to boost short-term profits – and destroyed the value of their brands. Brands that have come back from long declines are very rare.

4. Before marketers decide to aim for leadership in a particular market, they should consider if they are ready for a long war and indeed whether they want one. To start one, they need a high ad budget backed by large volume and a low cost structure. They may be better off modifying their ambitions and looking for market niches outside the spending wars. Clearly, the worst position is to be a midsize #3 competitor, not well differentiated from the leaders. Then all the economics work against you. ▽

Reprint 90113

Advertising and
Target Audiences

Beyond mass production and mass marketing to designer jeans and designer genes

Marketing in an Age of Diversity

by Regis McKenna

Spreading east from California, a new individualism has taken root across the United States. Gone is the convenient fiction of a single, homogeneous market. The days of a uniformly accepted view of the world are over. Today diversity exerts tremendous influence, both economically and politically.

Technology and social change are interdependent. Companies are using new flexible technology, like computer-aided design and manufacturing and software customization to create astonishing diversity in the marketplace and society. And individuals temporarily coalescing into "micromajorities" are making use of platforms—media, education, and the law—to express their desires.

In the marketing world, for example, the protests of thousands of consumers, broadcast by the media as an event of cultural significance, was enough to force Coca-Cola to reverse its decision to do away with "classic" Coke. On the political scene, vociferous minorities, sophisticated in using communication technology, exert influence greatly disproportionate to their numbers: the Moral Majority is really just another minority—but focused and amplified. When we see wealthy people driving Volkswagens and pickup trucks, it becomes clear that this is a society where individual tastes are no longer predictable; marketers cannot easily and neatly categorize their customer base.

Over the last 15 years, new technology has spawned products aimed at diverse, new sectors and market niches. Computer-aided technologies now allow companies to customize virtually any product, from designer jeans to designer genes, serving ever narrower customer needs. With this newfound technology, manufacturers are making more and more high-quality products in smaller and smaller batches; today 75% of all machined parts are produced in batches of 50 or fewer.

Consumers demand—and get—more variety and options in all kinds of products, from cars to clothes. Auto buyers, for example, can choose from 300 different types of cars and light trucks, domestic and imported, and get variations within each of those lines. Beer drinkers now have 400 brands to sample. The number of products in supermarkets has soared from

Regis McKenna is chairman of Regis McKenna Inc., a Palo Alto headquartered marketing company that advises some of America's leading high-tech companies. He is also a general partner of Kleiner Perkins Caufield & Byers, a technology venture-capital company. His book, The Regis Touch (Addison-Wesley), was published in 1985.

DRAWING BY PAUL MEISEL

13,000 in 1981 to 21,000 in 1987. There are so many new items that stores can demand hefty fees from packaged-foods manufacturers just for displaying new items on grocery shelves.

Deregulation has also increased the number of choices – from a flurry of competing airfares to automated banking to single-premium life insurance that you can buy at Sears. The government has even adapted antitrust laws to permit companies to serve emerging micromarkets: the Orphan Drug Act of 1983, for instance, gives pharmaceutical companies tax breaks and a seven-year monopoly on any drugs that serve fewer than 200,000 people.

Diversity and niches create tough problems for old-line companies more accustomed to mass markets. Sears, the country's largest retailer, is trying to reposition its products, which traditionally have appealed to older middle-class and blue-collar customers. To lure younger, style-minded buyers, Sears has come up with celebrity-signature lines, fashion boutiques, and a new line of children's clothing, McKids, playing off McDonald's draw. New, smaller stores, specialty catalogs, and merchandise tailored to regional tastes are all part of Sears's effort to reach a new clientele – and without alienating its old one.

Faced with slimmer profits from staples like detergents, diapers, and toothpaste, and lackluster results from new food and beverage products, Procter & Gamble, the world's largest marketer, is rethinking what it should sell and how to sell it. The company is now concentrating on health products; it has high hopes for a fat substitute called "olestra," which may take some of the junk out of junk food. At the same time that P&G is shifting its product thinking, it also is changing its organization, opening up and streamlining its highly insular pyramidal management structure as part of a larger effort to listen and respond to customers. Small groups that include both factory workers and executives work on cutting costs, while other teams look for new ways to speed products to market.

In trying to respond to the new demands of a diverse market, the problem that giants like Sears and P&G face is not fundamental change, not a total turnabout in what an entire nation of consumers wants. Rather, it is the fracturing of mass markets. To contend with diversity, managers must drastically alter how they design, manufacture, market, and sell their products.

Marketing in the age of diversity means:

☐ More options for goods producers and more choices for consumers.

☐ Less perceived differentiation among similar products.

☐ Intensified competition, with promotional efforts sounding more and more alike, approaching "white noise" in the marketplace.

☐ Newly minted meanings for words and phrases as marketers try to "invent" differentiation.

☐ Disposable information as consumers try to cope with information deluge from print, television, computer terminal, telephone, fax, satellite dish.

☐ Customization by users as flexible manufacturing makes niche production every bit as economic as mass production.

☐ Changing leverage criteria as economies of scale give way to economies of knowledge – knowledge of the customer's business, of current and likely future technology trends, and of the competitive environment that allows the rapid development of new products and services.

☐ Changing company structure as large corporations continue to downsize to compete with smaller niche players that nibble at their markets.

☐ Smaller wins—fewer chances for gigantic wins in mass markets, but more opportunities for healthy profits in smaller markets.

The Decline of Branding, the Rise of 'Other'

In today's fractured marketplace, tried-and-true marketing techniques from the past no longer work for most products—particularly for complex ones based on new technology. Branding products and seizing market share, for instance, no longer guarantee loyal customers. In one case after another, the old, established brands have been supplanted by the rise of "other."

Television viewers in 1983 and 1984, for instance, tuned out the big three broadcasters to watch cable and independent "narrowcast" stations. Last year, the trend continued as the big three networks lost 9% of their viewers—more than six million people. Small companies appealing to niche-oriented viewers attacked the majority market share. NBC responded by buying a cable television company for $20 million.

No single brand can claim the largest share of the gate array, integrated circuit, or computer market. Even IBM has lost its reign over the personal computer field—not to one fast-charging competitor but to an assortment of smaller producers. Tropicana, Minute Maid, and Citrus Hill actually account for less than half the frozen orange juice market. A full 56% belongs to hundreds of mostly small private labels. In one area after another, "other" has become the major market holder.

IBM's story of lost market share bears elaboration, in large part because of the company's almost legendary position in the U.S. business pantheon. After its rise in the personal computer market through 1984, IBM found its stronghold eroding—but not to just one, huge competitor that could be identified and stalked methodically. IBM could no longer rely on tracking the dozen or so companies that had been its steady competition for almost two decades. Instead, more than 300 clone producers worldwide intruded on Big Blue's territory. Moreover, IBM has faced the same competitive challenge in one product area after another, from supercomputers to networks. In response, IBM has changed how it does business. In the past, IBM wouldn't even bother to enter a market lacking a value of at least $100 million. But today, as customer groups diversify and markets splinter, that criterion is obsolete. The shift in competition has also prompted IBM to reorganize, decentralizing

the company into five autonomous groups so decisions can be made closer to customers.

Similar stories abound in other industries. Kodak dominated film processing in the United States until little kiosks sprang up in shopping centers and ate up that market. Twenty years ago, the U.S. semiconductor industry consisted of 100 companies; today there are more than 300. In fact, practically every industry has more of every kind of company catering to the consumer's love of diversity—more ice cream companies, more cookie companies, more weight loss and exercise companies. Last year, enterprising managers started 233,000 new businesses of all types to offer customers their choice of "other."

The False Security of Market Share

The proliferation of successful small companies dramatizes how the security of majority market share—seized by a large corporation and held unchallenged for decades—is now a dangerous anachronism. In the past, the dominant marketing models drew on the measurement and control notions embedded in engineering and manufacturing. The underlying mechanistic logic was that companies could measure everything, and anything they could measure, they could control—including customers. Market-share measurements became a way to understand the marketplace and thus to control it. For ex-

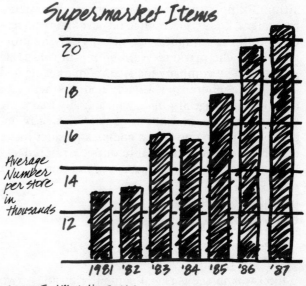

Source: Food Marketing Institute

Today's consumers have 60% more product variety in the supermarket than they did in 1981.

ample, marketers used to be able to pin down a target customer with relative ease: if it were a man, he was between 25 and 35 years old, married, with two-and-a-half children, and half a dog. Since he was one of so many measurable men in a mass society, marketers assumed that they could manipulate the market just by knowing the demographic characteristics.

But we don't live in that world anymore, and those kinds of measurements are meaningless. Marketers trying to measure that same "ideal" customer today would discover that the pattern no longer holds; that married fellow with two-and-a-half kids could now be divorced, situated in New York instead of Minnesota, and living in a condo instead of a brick colonial. These days, the idea of market share is a trap that can lull businesspeople into a false sense of security.

Managers should wake up every morning uncertain about the marketplace, because it is invariably changing. That's why five-year plans are dangerous: Who can pinpoint what the market will be five years from now? The president of one large industrial corporation recently told me, "The only thing we know about our business plan is that it's wrong. It's either too high or too low—but we never know which."

In the old days, mass marketing offered an easy solution: "just run some ads." Not today. IBM tried that approach with the PC JR., laying out an estimated $100 million on advertising—before the product failed. AT&T spent tens of millions of dollars running ads for its computer products.

In sharp contrast, Digital Equipment Corporation spent very little on expensive national television advertising and managed to wrest a healthy market position. Skipping the expensive mass-advertising campaigns, DEC concentrated on developing its reputation in the computer business by solving problems for niche markets. Word of mouth sold DEC products. The company focused its marketing and sales staffs where they already had business and aimed its message at people who actually make the decision on what machines to buy. DEC clearly understood that no one buys a complex product like a computer without a reliable outside reference—however elaborate the company's promotion.

Niche Marketing: Selling Big by Selling Small

Intel was in the personal computer business two years before Apple started in Steve Jobs's garage. The company produced the first microprocessor chip and subsequently developed an early version of what became known as the hobby computer, sold in electron-

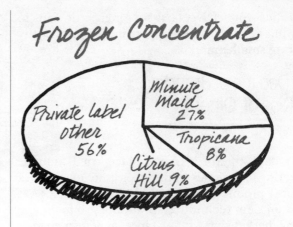

Data: Coca-Cola Foods
BCI Holdings, A.C. Nielsen Co.

The "big" brands aren't so big after all. "Other" is the market leader.

ics hobby stores. An early Intel advertisement in *Scientific American* showed a junior high school student using the product. Intel's market research, however, revealed that the market for hobbyists was quite small and it abandoned the project. Two years later, Apple built itself on the hobbyist market. As it turned out, many of the early users of personal computers in education, small business, and the professional markets came from hobbyists or enthusiasts.

I recently looked at several market forecasts made by research organizations in 1978 projecting the size of the personal computer market in 1985. The most optimistic forecast looked for a $2 billion market. It exceeded $25 billion.

Most large markets evolve from niche markets. That's because niche marketing teaches many important lessons about customers—in particular, to think of them as individuals and to respond to their special needs. Niche marketing depends on word-of-mouth references and infrastructure development, a broadening of people in related industries whose opinions are crucial to the product's success.

Infrastructure marketing can be applied to almost all markets. In the medical area, for example, recognized research gurus in a given field—diabetes, cancer, heart disease—will first experiment with new devices or drugs at research institutions. Universities and research institutions become identified by their specialties. Experts in a particular area talk to each other, read the same journals, and attend the same conferences. Many companies form their own scientific advisory boards designed to tap into the members' expertise and to build credibility for new technology and products. The word of mouth created by infrastructure marketing can make or break a new drug or a new supplier. Conductus, a new super-conductor company in Palo Alto, is building its business around an advisory board of seven top scientists from Stanford University and Berkeley.

Represented graphically, infrastructure development would look like an inverted pyramid. So Apple's pyramid, for instance, would include the references of influential users, software designers who create programs, dealers, industry consultants, analysts, the press, and, most important, customers.

Customer focus derived from niche marketing helps companies respond faster to demand changes. That is the meaning of today's most critical requirement – that companies become market driven. From the board of directors down through the ranks, company leaders must educate everyone to the singular importance of the customer, who is no longer a faceless, abstract entity or a mass statistic.

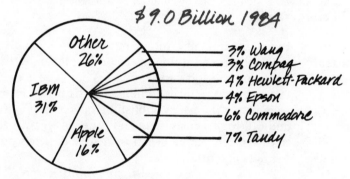

PC Market Share
(By Factory Revenue, U.S. only)

$9.0 Billion 1984

Other 26%
IBM 31%
Apple 16%

3% Wang
3% Compaq
4% Hewlett-Packard
4% Epson
6% Commodore
7% Tandy

Source: Future Computing, Inc. 1986

IBM led the market then...

Because niche markets are not easily identified in their infancy, managers must keep one foot in the technology to know its potential and one foot in the market to see opportunity. Tandem Computers built its solid customer base by adapting its products to the emerging on-line transaction market. Jimmy Treybig, president and CEO, told me that the company had to learn the market's language. Bankers don't talk about MIPS (millions of instructions per second) the way computer people do, he said; they talk about transactions. So Tandem built its products and marketing position to become the leading computer in the transaction market. Not long ago, Treybig was on a nationwide tour visiting key customers. "Guess who was calling on my customers just a few days ahead of me," he said. "John Akers" – chairman of IBM.

Many electronics companies have developed teams consisting of software and hardware development engineers, quality control and manufacturing people, as well as marketing and sales – who all visit customers or play key roles in dealing with customers. Convex Computer and Tandem use this approach. Whatever method a company may use, the purpose is the same: to get the entire company to focus on the fragmented, ever-evolving customer base as if it were an integral part of the organization.

The Integrated Product

Competition from small companies in fractured markets has even produced dramatic changes in how companies define their products. The product is no longer just the thing itself; it includes service, word-of-mouth references, company financial reports, the technology, and even the personal image of the CEO.

As a result, product marketing and service marketing, formerly two distinct fields, have become a single hybrid. For example, Genentech, which manufactures a growth hormone, arms its sales force with lap-top computers. When a Genentech salesperson visits an endocrinologist, the physician can tie into a data base of all the tests run on people with characteristics similar to his or her patients. The computer represents an extended set of services married to the original product.

Or take the example of Apple Computer and Quantum Corporation, which recently announced a joint venture offering on-line interactive computer services for Apple Computer users. In addition to a long list of transaction services that reads like a television programming guide, Apple product service, support, and even simple maintenance will be integrated into the product itself. Prodigy, a joint venture between IBM and Sears, will soon offer IBM and Apple users access to banking, shopping, the stock market, regional weather forecasts, sports statistics, encyclopedias of all kinds – and even direct advice from Sylvia Porter, Howard Cosell, or Ask Beth.

In consumer products, service has become the predominant distinguishing feature. Lands' End promotes its catalog-marketed outdoorsy clothes by guaranteeing products unconditionally and promising to ship orders within 24 to 48 hours. Carport, near Atlanta, offers air travelers an ultradeluxe parking service: it drives customers to their gates, checks their bags, and, while they are airborne, services, washes, and waxes their cars. "Macy's by Appointment" is a free shopping service for customers who are too busy or too baffled to make their own selections.

With so much choice backed by service, customers can afford to be fickle. As a result, references have become vital to product marketing. And the more complex the product, the more complex the supporting references. After all, customers who switch toothpaste risk losing only a dollar or so if the new choice is a dud. But consumers buying a complete phone system or a computer system or any other costly, long-term and pervasive product, cannot afford to take their investments lightly. References become a part of the product—and they come in all kinds of forms. Company financial reports are a kind of reference. A person shopping for an expensive computer wants to see how profitable the company is; how can the company promise maintenance service if it's about to fold? Even the CEO's personality can make a sale. Customers who see Don Petersen of Ford splashed across a magazine cover—or Apple's John Sculley or Hewlett-Packard's John Young—feel reassured that a real person stands behind the complex and expensive product.

In this complicated world, customers weigh all these factors to winnow out the products they want from those they don't. Now more than ever, marketers must sell every aspect of their businesses as important elements of the products themselves.

The Customer As Customizer

Customer involvement in product design has become an accepted part of the development and marketing processes in many industries. In technologically driven products, which often evolve slowly as discoveries percolate to the surface, the customer can practically invent the market for a company.

Apple's experience with desktop publishing shows how companies and customers work together to create new applications—and new markets. Apple entered the field with the Macintosh personal computer, which offered good graphics and easy-to-use features. But desktop publishing didn't even exist then; it wasn't on anyone's pie chart as a defined market niche, and no one had predicted its emergence.

Apple's customers made it happen; newspapers and research organizations simply started using Macintosh's unique graphics capability to create charts and graphs. Early users made do with primi-

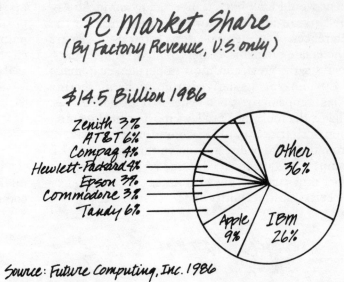

PC Market Share (By Factory Revenue, U.S. only)

$14.5 Billion 1986

Zenith 3%
AT&T 6%
Compaq 4%
Hewlett-Packard 4%
Epson 3%
Commodore 3%
Tandy 6%

Other 36%
Apple 9%
IBM 26%

Source: Future Computing, Inc. 1986

...but now it's been eclipsed by clone companies it can't identify or stalk.

tive software and printers, but that was enough to spark the imagination of other developers. Other hardware and software companies began developing products that could be combined with the Macintosh to enhance the user's publishing power. By visiting and talking to customers and other players in the marketplace, Apple began to realize desktop publishing's potential.

As customers explored the possibilities presented by the technology, the technology, in turn, developed to fit the customers' needs. The improved software evolved from a dynamic working relationship between company and customers, not from a rigid, bureaucratic headquarters determination of where Apple could find an extra slice of the marketing pie.

Technological innovation makes it easier to involve customers in design. For example, Milliken, the textile manufacturer, provides customers with computer terminals where they can select their own carpet designs from thousands of colors and patterns. Electronics customers, too, have assumed the role of product designer. New design tools allow companies like Tandem and Convex to design their own specialty chips, which the integrated-circuit suppliers then manufacture according to their specifications. Similarly, American Airlines designs its own computer systems. In cases like these, the design and manufacturing processes have been completely separated. So semiconductor companies – and many computer companies – have become raw-materials producers, with integration occurring all the way up the supply line.

The fact that customers have taken charge of design opens the door for value-added resellers, who integrate different materials and processes. These people are the essence of new-age marketers: they add value by understanding what happens in a doctor's office or a travel agency or a machine-tool plant and customize that service or product to the customer's needs. To capitalize on market changes, companies should follow these examples and work directly with customers – even before products hit the drawing boards.

The Evolution of Distribution

It's nearly impossible to make a prediction on the basis of past patterns. Perhaps many big institutions founded on assumptions of mass marketing and market share will disappear like dinosaurs. Or they'll evolve into closely integrated service and distribution organizations.

In fact, tremendous innovation in distribution channels has already begun in nearly every industry. Distribution channels have to be flexible to survive. As more flows into them, they have to change. Grocery stores sell flowers and cameras. Convenience stores rent out videos. And television offers viewers direct purchasing access to everything from diamonds to snowblowers to a decent funeral.

To get products closer to customers, marketers are distributing more and more samples in more ways. Today laundry detergent arrives in the mail, magazines enfold perfume-doused tear-outs, and department stores offer chocolate samples. Software companies bind floppy disk samples into magazines or mail out diskettes that work only until a certain date, giving customers the chance to test a product before buying.

Every successful computer retailer has not only a showroom but also a classroom. The large computer retailers are not selling to just off-the-street traffic. Most of their volume now comes from a direct sales force calling on corporate America. In addition, all have application-development labs, extensive user-training programs and service centers – and some have recently experimented with private labeling their own computer product brands. The electronics community talks more and more about design centers – places where customers can get help customizing products and applications.

Today the product is an experience. As customers use it, they grow to trust it – and distribution represents the beginning of that evolving relationship. That's why computer companies donate their systems to elementary schools: schools are now a distribution channel for product experience.

Goliath plus David

Besides making changes in distribution channels, big corporations will also have to forge new partnerships with smaller companies. IBM, for example, already has ties to 1,500 small computer-service companies nationwide, offering help for IBM mid-sized machine owners. Olivetti makes personal computers for AT&T. All over the world, manufacturers are producing generic computer platforms; larger companies buy these, then add their own service-oriented, value-adding applications.

This approach seems almost inevitable considering what we know about patterns of research and development. Technological developments typically originate with basic research, move to applied research, to development, then to manufacturing and marketing. Very few U.S. companies do basic research; universities and various public and private labs generally shoulder that burden. Many big companies do applied R&D while small companies concentrate on development. Basic and applied research means time and money. Consider the cases of two seminal inventions – antibiotics and television – the first of which took 30 years and the second 63 years from idea to the market.

Perhaps because of their narrow focus, small companies realize more development breakthroughs than larger ones. For example, the origins of recombinant DNA technology go back to the mid-1950s; it took Genentech only about six years to bring the world's first recombinant DNA commercial product to market.

A 1986 study by the Small Business Administration showed that 55% of innovations have come from companies with fewer than 500 employees, and twice as many innovations per employee come from small companies than from large ones. This finding, however, does not indicate that large companies are completely ineffective developers. Rather, the data suggest that small, venture-capitalized companies will scramble to invent a product that the market does not yet want, need, or perhaps even recognize; big companies will wait patiently for the market to develop so they can enter later with their strong manufacturing and marketing organizations.

The Japanese have shown us that it's wise to let small companies handle development–but only if large companies can somehow share that wisdom before the product reaches the market. From 1950 to 1978, Japanese companies held 32,000 licensing agreements to acquire foreign technology–mostly from the United States–for about $9 billion. In essence, the Japanese simply subcontracted out for R&D–and then used that investment in U.S. knowledge to dominate one market after another.

If orchestrated properly, agreements between large and small companies can prove mutually beneficial. When Genentech developed its first product, recombinant DNA insulin, the company chose not to compete against Eli Lilly, which held over 70% of the insulin market. Instead, Genentech entered into a licensing agreement with Lilly that put the larger company in charge of manufacturing and marketing the products developed by the smaller company. Over time, Genentech built its own manufacturing company while maintaining its proprietary product.

This model worked so well that it has shaped the fortunes of Silicon Valley. Of the 3,000 companies there, only a dozen hold places on the lists of America's largest corporations. Most of the companies are small developers of new products. Like the Japanese, large U.S. companies are now subcontracting development to these mostly high-tech startups. In the process, they are securing a critical resource–an ongoing relationship with a small, innovative enterprise.

Giant companies can compete in the newly diversifying markets if they recognize the importance of relationships–with small companies, within their own organizations, with their customers. Becoming market driven means abandoning old-style marketshare thinking and instead tying the uniqueness of any product to the unique needs of the customer. This approach to marketing demands a revolution in how businesspeople act–and even more important, in how they think. These changes are critical to success, but they can come only gradually, as managers and organizations adapt to the new rules of marketing in the age of diversity. As any good marketer knows, even instant success takes time.

Reprint 88511

"I'm sorry, but Mr. Connolly is not yet up to speed."

Critical issues for issue ads

David Kelley

*How—without even knowing it—
companies allow
their opponents
to set the ground rules
for their ideological battles
in the media*

U.S. companies get high marks for being concerned enough about public opinion to wage campaigns of advocacy, or issue, advertising in many newspapers. Often placed on the editorial page, these boxes are becoming well known as a sounding board in which business can show a "human side" by discussing everything from the excess oil profits tax to "Masterpiece Theatre." The ads may infuriate some and tickle others, but at least, say their advocates, companies have come out of the closet and aren't afraid to "take their case before the American people."

Despite their flashy campaigns, their big budgets, and a lot of intercompany backslapping, some companies are not pleased with the results. They complain that the message is still not getting across, that whatever their good intentions, they fail in the end.

It's not that companies aren't discussing the right issues, because they are. It's not that they don't speak in language that can be understood, because they do. No, according to David Kelley, companies do not make much headway with these campaigns because they use terms and a frame of reference that are fundamentally antibusiness. Companies are starting out from a position of inherent weakness instead of strength. Unless they change the way they state their case, it doesn't matter what they are trying to say. Here, Kelley explains just what companies are doing wrong and what they can do about it.

Mr. Kelley has written widely on business and economic issues, especially for Barron's. *His commentary on business and the media appeared in the* SmithKline Forum *in 1981, and he participated in the Media Institute's recent conference on the same subject. He is assistant professor of philosophy at Vassar College, where he teaches political philosophy and logic.*

Concerned about what they see as a bias against business in the media, U.S. companies are increasingly taking their message on basic issues directly to the consumer. Company spokesmen use sophisticated techniques to package and target the message in issue advertising. But, as is the case with much advertising, they often pay too much attention to the form and too little to the content of the message.

Consider an ad by Amway Corporation —the one discussing the impact of government regulation on all of us and picturing the federal government as the nanny shown in the *Exhibit* on page 84. It has a provocative subject. It reads well. It's visually forceful, if a little unsubtle. But is it effective? And worth the price of the space it will take? To find out, let's look closely at the text.

"We used to worry about Big Brother. Now, there's a real threat—the Federal Nanny. She's everywhere." This opener is right on target, we might say. Government regulation of business *is* an issue of freedom.

Amway's use of the Big Brother image is a good idea, for it points up the danger that extreme regulation poses. But regulators don't wear jackboots; they wear good, sensible shoes. And most Americans have no experience of the midnight knock on the door; their pride and independence make ridicule more effective than any appeal to fear. So Amway brings the subject to the more appropriate image of a nanny.

"Over-regulation increases your cost of living." This paragraph shifts our attention from our pride to our pocketbooks. It's a little jarring, but the ad succeeds here by asking us to think about the issue in personal terms: $2,000 per family is a lot of money. We'd like to decide for ourselves how to spend it, and we can appreciate business people not liking being told how to do their jobs. This perspective puts the company and the reader on the same footing and the burden on the regulators to justify their intrusions into the lives of ordinary citizens. The argument of this paragraph is effective.

But notice what happens in the next: the ad asks us to shift from our own perspective to that of a legislator. "Some people feel more secure with this kind of government 'protection,' and, of course, some government regulation is necessary. But it's gone too far." Well, we might say, I don't need a nanny, but others might. Maybe some regulation *is* necessary. If even companies say that some government regulation is necessary, it must be true. Maybe Nader's right. How much regulation do we need? Amway says it's gone too far because it comes to $105 billion. That's a lot of money—but the government spends a lot more on military defense, and no one calls it a nanny on that account. Maybe $105 billion is reasonable, but how do I know whether it is?

An important—if subtle—shift in perspective has occurred, one that alters the way "regulation" looks to the reader. At first, the simple image of a nanny, when amplified by a discussion of the impact of regulation on the individual's standard of living, easily conveys the problem with regulation: it takes away the freedom of responsible adults.

But then, the change of perspective destroys the impact of the advertising and shows just how companies can undermine their own messages. Once the ad allows that some regulation is necessary, it gives credence to the claims of business's critics. It also turns the issue into a matter of degree: how much regulation? The ad cannot possibly offer the lengthy analysis necessary to justify its position on this issue, so the position comes across as arbitrary, leaving the reader unmoved at best and probably suspicious: what has happened here, and why?

If we can judge by numerous corporate advocacy campaigns, speeches by top executives, and discussions in business publications, the defenders of business feel constrained to operate within a framework for discussion that is skewed against the free market system and corporate enterprise. Simply put, the critics of corporations have been allowed to set the terms of the debate in which everything concerning business is argued.

Accepting this framework is a fundamental mistake. Philosophy has long taught that assumptions granted at the outset of any argument help determine the success or failure of a particular point of view. These assumptions set the framework for argument and determine how the issue is stated, who has the burden of proof, what facts are relevant and how they are evaluated, which arguments seem convincing and which miss the point, what questions

critics will ask and what they will accept as valid answers.

Unless business challenges the fundamental assumptions that define the framework in which we currently debate social and economic issues, it can expect nothing more than occasional local victories in the marketplace of ideas—bull rallies in a primarily bear market. I think this challenge should begin with a look at the three most important assumptions made:

1   The public interest is the ultimate standard by which we are to judge everything, including business.

2   Since it is founded on the pursuit of material wealth, business has a lower moral value than other activities.

3   Since it is subject to political controls, a company is a political as well as an economic entity.

Understanding these assumptions will help solve the difficulty business has had in making an effective case. Let's look at each in turn to find where they come from, how they structure the logic of debate, and how companies can avoid them.

Individual rights & the public interest

The argument most commonly offered in defense of business is that it serves the public interest, primarily by creating jobs and goods that consumers want. The moral assumption is that the public interest is the ultimate standard by which we are to judge social issues.

A Citibank ad proclaims that "the American economic system is based on the premise that the public benefits from free competition and suffers from its absence." United Technology says that "we need unity of purpose and a sense of pulling together toward goals serving the broad public interest." Du Pont's former chairman Irving Shapiro is encouraged to see a growing public awareness that "business is not the enemy of society but is simply its instrument."[1] *Fortune* editor Paul Weaver argues that "business needs to develop the ability to take positions that embody a clear notion of the public interest."[2]

The problem with such arguments is not that they are false. By any reasonable standard, a free market economy does serve the public interest.

---

1 From a Wharton symposium, quoted in *Business Week*, April 13, 1981, p. 13.

2 See "Corporations are Defending Themselves with the Wrong Image," *Fortune*, June 1977, p. 194.

The problem lies with the implication. The argument boils down to the old advice not to kill the goose that lays the golden eggs. That's good advice—unless you happen to be the goose, in which case you might want a stronger foundation for your right to exist than the expediency of your masters. In other words, the appeal to the public interest implies that business people are second-class citizens who must justify their existence and that they can do that only by serving others.

The basis for the argument comes from social critics of the nineteenth century who embraced a collectivist view of society, in which the public interest stands above private interests. In German philosophy and later in the American Progressive and Pragmatist movements, private interest even became a term of opprobrium. Utilitarians like John Stuart Mill talked of the duty to pursue the greatest happiness of the greatest number. They did not tie the public interest to the preservation of individual rights; on the contrary, they considered individual freedom a privilege that society grants and intends for service to the public good. This is the antithesis of the individualist philosophy espoused by thinkers like John Locke and Thomas Jefferson. In that philosophy, individual rights are primary; the public interest is simply the common interest we all have in preserving the framework of rights.

Statements linking business with the public interest without mentioning rights clearly invoke this collectivist framework and will naturally work against any argument for economic freedom that is made within it.

The history of social thought is littered with examples of how this works. Consider Andrew Carnegie's essay of 1889, "The Gospel of Wealth." In response to populist hostility toward the large corporation, Carnegie and other industrialists cast themselves in the role of the stewards of society's capital. Carnegie said that the moral imperative for those who acquire great wealth is to administer it "for the highest good of the people," to distribute the surplus in accordance with the general welfare. The moral justification for allowing wealth to accumulate in private hands in the first place, he claimed, is that in a free market, only those who can use wealth productively are able to acquire it. The market selects the best stewards. According to Carnegie, then, wealth belongs by right to society and must be used for its benefit.

Critics of capitalism, from social scientists like Lester Ward to Progressive philosophers like Herbert Croly, took the ball from there. They argued that if the wealth is society's, then its stewards must be accountable to the public. This argument became a key intellectual basis for the first wave of political controls over business—central banking, antitrust laws, and the early regulatory agencies.

Today companies occasionally use Carnegie's argument (although they don't call it the "gospel of wealth"), and it still plays into the hands of those who clamor for corporate accountability. But let's look at two other, more recent issues in which the same logic is at work—cost-benefit analysis and profits.

Cost-benefit analysis

Companies have won some of their battles against regulatory agencies largely because of the cost-benefit studies that economists have made of various regulations over the past 20 years. Murray Weidenbaum's estimate of $100 billion as the indirect cost of regulation has through endless repetition become a fixture in public debate. Even the Environmental Protection Agency, the group least affected by the pressure for deregulation, cannot assign infinite value to goods like clean air or impose limitless costs on industry.

Companies may win this battle but lose the war. A case for business freedom cannot rest on cost-benefit analysis alone, or the gold mine becomes a land mine. Cost-benefit analysis is inherently collectivist because it measures the public good and defines it as the sum of all benefits and costs to everyone affected by a certain action. Any argument based on it is simply a more precise version of the appeal to the public interest.

Critics of the market are happy to have this collectivist standard accepted as the criterion for forming social policy. At some point, they find it quite easy to reject the economist's definition of the public good. After all, cost-benefit analysis relies on market prices to quantify costs and benefits. What it measures is therefore the sum of values that individuals place on goods. Unless we accept the individual's right to choose values and to pursue them, we cannot accept cost-benefit measures. Advocates of regulation already attack them on precisely this ground.

How do we establish a right? Not by cost-benefit arguments. We never subject the rights to freedom of speech and press, for example, to this sort of test. If we did, we would have lost them long ago. We accept the right to intellectual freedom because man's nature as an autonomous intellectual being requires it. Rights to property and contract have the same kind of basis: by our nature, we need autonomy in economic as well as intellectual matters.

A Citibank ad put it well: we are "intelligent beings whose nature requires us to be free agents." Once companies campaign to have these rights accepted, they can use cost-benefit analysis in particular areas of the economy to determine whether the market effectively integrates the activities of individuals exercising their rights. But companies cannot reverse that logical order.

Profits immoral?

Moral attitudes toward business crystallize around the subject of profit, and profit takes on a distinct moral color in each framework.

In fact, business provides an array of benefits – to consumers, a range of products they could not otherwise enjoy, at prices they are willing to pay; to workers, a way of supporting themselves productively, at wages that make it worth their while; to investors, a return on the capital they put up at risk. From an individualist standpoint, each of these benefits has the same moral status: each benefit is good for the party who receives it, and that people can cooperate to their mutual benefit is good for everyone. To put it another way, it is no more to be expected – it would no more be right – for investors to undertake risk without return than it would be for workers to work without pay or for consumers to pay for things they did not want.

Collectivism, however, takes for granted the benefits to both workers and consumers. They are the public, and business merely does its duty to serve the public when it renders services to them. Collectivists see profits as a loss to society: without them, goods would be cheaper and wages higher than they are. That is precisely what the socialists have hoped to achieve by abolishing profit. But it doesn't work that way economically. Companies know that without profits, no one puts up the capital to make the other benefits possible. If they don't challenge this collectivist moral assumption, the fundamental economic fact appears as a necessary evil, a concession to the greed of business people.

Accepting the collectivist assumption by stressing the social benefits of the profit motive or pointing out how low profits are – the two points about profit that issue ads make most often – simply backfires. In effect, the message of companies to the public is: "We wouldn't serve you at all without taking something for ourselves from the public till, and besides we don't take much." That message only encourages opposition to profit, even among those who understand its economic role. When the windfall profits tax was proposed, for example, no one pretended that it made any economic sense; with the doubtful exception of President Carter, no one really believed that the proceeds would trickle down to consumers. But the tax was absolutely unavoidable in the face of the moral hysteria over oil company profits. Despite heroic efforts to enlighten the public about the economic necessity of their profits, the oil companies did nothing to dispel the public's hostility.

Companies fear they will antagonize the public by vigorously defending corporate self-interest, but challenging the public interest ideology need not backfire. The secret lies in the way companies put their message across.

Everyone knows that the profit motive is not altruistic, and a clear acknowledgment of that fact would at least demonstrate corporate credibility. More important, Americans are not collectivists at heart, and it is possible to tap into their sense of individualism and independence with a message that reads, in effect: "You wouldn't put in a full day's work unless your contribution was recognized with a full day's pay. We won't either. Last year we made X in profit, and we're proud of every cent. Here's what we did to earn it."

The moral nature of enterprise

If business wants to make an effective case for itself, it must also challenge the second assumption, that business is materialistic. The assumption takes many different forms. The root idea is that material wealth has a lower value than art, knowledge, or spiritual fulfillment. This evaluation spreads to activities of production and trade and makes them seem routine, mechanical, mundane, and uninspiring.

Although a moment's thought makes it obvious that business success depends as much on intelligence as does anything else, the public does not consider business an intellectual activity. Nor does it see business offering much room for individuality: in the popular image, executives are faceless and interchangeable. Even sympathizers think that business encourages the "bourgeois" virtues of rationality, industriousness, and financial rectitude and discourages the more "heroic" virtues of imagination, vision, passionate commitment, integrity in the face of pressure, and courage in the face of risk.

These attitudes have had a varied life in our culture. The animus toward material values is a heritage of religious traditions that emphasize the otherworldly: even the Puritan fathers of "the work ethic" prided themselves on "loving the world with weaned affections." The secular philosophers of the Enlightenment looked with favor on the motive of economic self-interest, but they did so because they considered it dispassionate and thus safer than the motive of personal glory, which inflames politics. That was the thrust of Samuel Johnson's remark that "there are few ways in which a man can be more innocently employed than in getting money"; commerce isn't noble, in other words, but at least it does no harm.

The Federal Nanny.

Domestic help we can't afford.

We used to worry about Big Brother. Now, there's a real threat—the Federal Nanny.

She's everywhere—regulating everything from ladders to land use. She inspects small business for the tiniest violations; she sets prices for energy production; she decides which expensive "refinements" will adorn the family car.

Over-regulation increases your cost of living. In 1979 it will cost each U.S. family about $2,000—a good start toward buying a new car! You see, it takes almost $5 billion to keep the regulators working in Washington. And business must spend $100 billion to comply with the regulations. Here's the catch...because those billions produce no more goods for sale, the costs are added to every product you buy.

Some people feel more secure with this kind of government "protection", and, of course, some government regulation is necessary. But it's gone too far. Nowadays, the Federal Nanny wants to run the whole house! Trouble is, we can't afford it.

In the last several years, the ideas of government regulators have added more than $600 to the price of a new car. Was it worth it?

We can all realize *substantial* savings if we all depend less on that expensive Nanny from Washington. Amway Corporation, Ada, MI., 49355.

Amway®

One of a series of messages to stimulate public dialogue about significant national issues.

Romantic thinkers rebelled against what they saw as the unheroic character of bourgeois virtues. Their attitude reappeared in the 1950s image of the organization man and the 1960s talk about alienation.

Business people allow these attitudes to flourish more by silence than by active assent. Perhaps this silence comes from modesty, perhaps from a pragmatic belief that nothing so intangible can make any practical impact. If that is what business people believe, however, they are making a mistake. We have only to look as far as the issue of regulation to see the results of these attitudes.

Here again, we can learn something by comparing economic with intellectual freedom. Journalists defend the freedom of the press in part by arguing that competition among ideas helps ensure that truth prevails over error—just as business argues that competition in the marketplace tends to ensure that good products and honest practices predominate. The arguments are exactly parallel.

Yet freedom of speech is more secure in this country than economic freedom. One reason is that, when threatened, journalists do not rely solely on the argument that competition promotes quality but rather cast the issue as an assault on the mind, an attempt to suppress their integrity as individuals. They invoke the tradition of heroic thinkers standing alone against orthodoxy and popular prejudice. Freedom itself becomes the central issue, and it moves us because a long line of victims, from Socrates to Solzhenitsyn, have shown what human qualities the loss of liberty would destroy.

Business freedom, in contrast, remains largely an abstraction. The popular mind has no sense of what human qualities this principle protects.

Business has never pointed out that what the government regulates is people and that regulation is a way of censoring their ideas, their values, and their imaginations. As a result, regulation is seen as only one of the devices governing that vast, mechanical, impersonal machine we call the economy; arguments that the device does not work well do not inspire outrage even when they convince. The Amway ad begins to make this point with its image of the federal nanny but quickly drops the point and returns to the usual cost-benefit approach to regulation.

So those attitudes are potent. Business could take various concrete measures to counter them. The first is to respond effectively to hostile portrayals of business in the media. A recent study done by the Media Institute found that in two out of three cases television presents business people as foolish or evil;

nearly half the business activities shown are illicit. Business's response to the study never quite hit the mark. A United Technology ad, for example, wound up its discussion of the study with two ironies—that TV is itself a business and that business advertising supports it. In logic, that sort of reply is known as a *tu quoque* ("you're another!"), and it is a fallacy: you can't refute one insult with another.

United Technology probably avoided a more direct rebuttal for fear the public would say it was blowing its own horn. That fear is unnecessary. There is a perfectly simple, dignified, effective response to make in this context: TV writers and producers would never allow themselves to treat blacks, or women, or school teachers, or any other group with such blind hostility. Should they be any less ashamed of their prejudice toward people in business?

A second measure for companies to take is to launch programs in economic education. The programs that now exist tend to focus on how the economy works as a whole. This effort is all to the good, for the public has become familiar with the standard economic terms and even with the reason that government regulation adversely affects business. What is missing is an idea of what goes on *inside* the corporations that compete in the market. Without this, it is natural for people to think of business, especially big business, as a kind of impersonal machine. They need to see real people at work on real problems within companies. Public television's new series "Enterprise" has so far had several episodes that illustrate the sort of thing I mean: without sentimentalizing their subject, the producers make business engrossing and dramatic.

The most important measure, however, is to speak out about government interference in business life in a very personal way. When Sohio announced that it was abandoning its California-Texas pipeline for Alaskan crude in 1979 because of regulatory delay and the threat of further litigation, the public was surprised—surprised by the unmistakable note of weary frustration in the company's statement; surprised by the unprecedented revelation that business is not a workhorse that will plod along no matter what burdens the public authorities place on it.

This kind of revelation ought to occur more often. Regulations have driven companies out of business and subjected whole industries to a kind of prior restraint, an assumption of guilt until innocence is proven. Where is the outrage at such injustice? In private conversation, business people speak with bitterness of talented people giving up in frustration and of innovations drowning in a sea of paperwork; but official statements are normally couched in colorless terms of costs and benefits, drained of all moral force. Business can no longer afford this sort of gray silence about its own victimization.

Editor's note: Amway Corporation does not agree with the author's analysis of the advocacy advertisement on the facing page and thus provides it to HBR so that our readers will have the opportunity to read both the article and the ad and to decide for themselves whether the analysis is reasonable.

Corporations as political entities

The third assumption skewing the case for business concerns the corporation as a social institution. Writers on the left have labored hard to erase the distinction between economic and political power by portraying large corporations, which undeniably possess great economic power, as political entities that should be subject to popular control. John Kenneth Galbraith has argued that while small companies are competitive and genuinely private, large corporations possess something like political power in their ability to "administer" prices, mold public opinion, and influence the government. The New Left, fundamentally opposed to capitalism and the profit motive, has nevertheless waxed eloquent about the virtues of small entrepreneurial enterprise in order to rail against the power of big business.

The reason the Left wants to blur the line between business and politics is obvious. If we can apply to business the conceptual framework in which we view government, then we can control business power the way we do government power. That is the premise behind Ralph Nader's drive to "constitutionalize" the corporation and related proposals for corporate democracy.

A democratic system cannot tolerate any permanent concentration of political power in private hands – or anything it perceives as such. Business freedom can be preserved only if corporations are seen as voluntary associations among individuals in pursuit of noncoercive ends. If corporations are classified with government as agents of coercive power, then the framework of rights will necessarily be applied against them. Indeed, this pattern is occurring already in regard to worker and consumer rights.

Consumers are demanding that products be safe to use and reliable. Workers want variety and autonomy in the workplace. One way or the other, business will have to deal with these pressures, but it can make a difference only by framing the issues properly. If public demands are accepted as rights against the corporation, then workers and consumers will not hesitate to enlist the aid of government in securing them. That is what government is for, after all – to secure our rights. But these demands on companies cannot be rights. Someone must produce reliable goods. To claim a right to them is to claim a right to the efforts of those who produce the goods – no one has such rights against other people.

Companies can make this negative and deflating point in a positive way. In the first place, corporations compete for customers and employees and have every incentive to provide as much of what they want as is economically possible. Product competition with the Japanese, for example, has spawned various experiments in worker participation. Second, people differ in what they want. Some consumers want more safety features in products than others do. Consumer advocates trumpet these demands as the norm, but many people don't want to pay the higher price of added safety for all products, a point well dramatized by Monte Throdahl in a tongue-in-cheek issue ad about a $17 pencil. This excellent ad showed what would happen to the price of pencils if consumer advocates got worried about the dangers of these sharply pointed objects.[3] In the same way, some workers prefer the chance for rapid advancement in a growing company that cannot afford the job-security benefits of an already established corporation. Everyone is better off if all parties are free to work out cooperative arrangements on a voluntary, individualistic basis. A government-enforced "bill of rights," in contrast, would impose a uniform standard – satisfactory at best to a bare majority – and ensure that neither workers nor consumers would ever receive more than the legal minimum.

A second and equally pressing issue is the alleged political influence of business. Several years ago, an opinion research project organized by Louis Banks at the Massachusetts Institute of Technology's Sloan School found that "the only point of sharp conflict [between journalists and business executives] came in questions about the *power* of business in American life. The corporation executives believe that business has very little power, and the journalists believe strongly that business has too much."[4] We can understand the difference in opinion by looking at benchmarks against which the two groups measure results. Journalists often assume that government has an unlimited right to control economic activity and thus see business success in escaping controls as an exercise of power against the public will.

As Robert Hessen has shown,[5] that was the implicit argument of Charles V. Lindblom's influential book *Politics and Markets:*[6] if they are still free to operate as private entities, corporations must have manipulated the political process and even popular opinion so as to prevent the political control over them that would otherwise have occurred by now.

Business executives, on the other hand, naturally see any success as an act of self-defense, an attempt to ward off injury rather than gain positive

3 See "The Pencil Problem – 1990,"
   Milliken & Company, New York.

4 See Louis Banks,
   "Taking on the Hostile Media,"
   HBR March-April 1978, p. 123.

5 See *Does Big Business Rule America?*
   (Washington, D.C.:
   Ethics and Public Policy Center, 1981).

6 *Politics and Markets:*
   The World's Political-Economic Systems
   (New York: Basic Books, 1977).

7 See "What Is Business Ethics?"
   The Public Interest,
   Spring 1981, p. 18.

benefits from the political process. In this light, business is not very powerful. Consider the areas of alleged influence. With some notable exceptions, such as the milk producers, most lobbying has only limited the damage of antibusiness legislation. Regulatory agencies have in some cases been captured by the industries over which they were supposed to serve as watchdogs – older, industry-based agencies like the ICC and the FCC. But the government is currently deregulating these very industries.

Newer agencies like the EPA and OSHA have functional mandates ranging across the economy, and industry certainly hasn't captured them. Finally, as Peter Drucker has noted, many of the widely publicized cases of corporate bribery and illicit campaign contributions are really cases of extortion by government officials wielding discretionary power over business.[7]

I do not want to make the waters seem less muddy than they are, but to the extent that business's political activities have been defensive, it is important for business to stress the point. As many commentators have observed, a strong vein of populism makes Americans easy prey for theories about the political conspiracies of large corporations. But there is an equally strong feeling for the democratic right to have one's interests represented in Washington and for the constitutional right to petition government for a redress of grievances. These are possible bases of popular sympathy for business. Whether companies can earn that sympathy depends on how the public measures the true nature of their political influence, and that depends on which conceptual framework companies bring into play.

self-interest as evil and the pursuit of wealth as dangerous or dishonorable. These are the attitudes that have impeded progress in the developing nations and that are struggling for ascendancy in the West.

If business leaves these attitudes unchallenged, the growth in political control over the economy will continue unabated and the corporation will not have to worry about its external relations: it will simply dissolve into its political environment. The offices and trademarks may remain, but the corporation as a locus of genuinely private decision making will gradually disappear.

Second, companies should not assume the inevitability of an antibusiness ideology. The current environment is largely the product of anticapitalist ideas that have flourished among intellectuals for a century and been absorbed by the "new class" of journalists, foundation executives, public-sector professionals, and the like. Assuming that intellectuals are necessarily antibusiness or anticapitalist is a sociological fallacy. Those attitudes are the product of historical trends, and they are subject to change. Indeed, small but promising signs of change are already showing up in a new generation of economic and political theorists. Change is slow at these altitudes, however, and the process by which new ideas trickle down, slower still. Business could speed things up by putting some new ideas to use now.

Thus, it is both possible and desirable for business to become active in approaching the ideological environment – at least to the extent of insisting on a framework of discussion that is hospitable to the case it tries to make in its own communications to the public. ▽

Reprint 82408

Mistaken policies

It has commonly been said, especially in standard texts for "Business and Society" courses, that external corporate relations will be an important, perhaps the most important, function of management in coming years. But the observation usually implies that the political and ideological environment is a given to which business must adapt. In the short run, this is doubtless true. But as the basis for a long-range policy, it is mistaken on two counts.

First, we should not assume that business can adapt to any environment just by being nimble and pragmatic. The capitalist system and its private, voluntary organizations have existed only in the last 200 years and only in a few countries. They cannot survive indefinitely in a culture with a collectivist outlook, in a culture that regards the pursuit of

When to advertise your company

*Primarily
when you wish to be remembered
or understood,
but not if you hope to
fool the public*

Thomas F. Garbett

Corporate advertising goes beyond public relations and beyond product or brand advertising. Its aims include creating a lasting and favorable impression of a company and establishing a corporate identity. Although it cannot long maintain a false image, it can succeed when its goal is to correct a misinformed viewpoint or to ensure that a company is remembered. And in industries prone to criticism involving environmental issues or other public concerns, corporate campaigns can work to build credibility.

The author's exploration of corporate advertising is founded on his survey of 750 major corporations. He examines reasons for and against this advertising and provides guidelines managers can consult when determining whether they should launch corporate advertising programs.

Mr. Garbett is senior vice president and management supervisor at Doyle Dane Bernbach Inc., the New York advertising agency. Among the industries in which he has served as an advertising specialist are automobiles and packaged goods. His book, Corporate Advertising: The What, the Why and the How, *was published by McGraw-Hill in 1981.*

Photograph by Ralph Mercer.

When it comes to deciding whether to institute corporate advertising programs, major corporations are far from being in agreement. Of the nation's 500 largest industrial companies, 244 opted for such programs in 1980 while 256 did not use them. Thus they split nearly down the middle.

Why do some companies have corporate ad programs while others shy away from them? On what logical or illogical grounds is that decision based?

In this article, I discuss which companies and industries use corporate advertising, why they do so, and under what conditions it's beneficial. As part of the research for the article, I surveyed corporate advertising expenditures among the *Fortune "500"* industrial and "250" nonindustrial companies. (The ruled insert on page 106 contains a more detailed description of the survey.) Beyond the survey, I have determined from experience and close observation many company and industry factors that are associated with use of corporate advertising.

Before considering what criteria companies should use when deciding about corporate ads, let's examine more closely what such advertising entails. Campaigns formerly called public opinion advertising, institutional advertising, or image advertising can be considered corporate advertising—media space or time bought for the benefit of the corporation rather than its products or services. Such advertising may be divided into three major categories: issue or advocacy advertising, financial- or investor-relations programs, and general corporate image building.

Issue advertising. Companies usually conduct issue advertising in response to what they consider to be threatening legislative or social activity. When a corporation speaks up and presents its side in a controversy, benefits accrue not only to the company but to the public as well, because a more complete evaluation becomes possible. But far more prevalent than controversial presentations are programs in which companies champion popular ideas, either to gain attention or to give evidence of their concern. Even topics like deregulation, tax-law reform, new legislation, or tariffs may be handled within the scope of safe corporate advertising.

Financial-relations advertising. This advertising can stimulate the interest of potential investors. There are just too many companies and too few analysts to ensure fair and equal evaluation of all companies—particularly smaller concerns. Analysts gain little additional information from corporate ads, but the portrait of a company on the move and doing exciting things may influence their thinking.

Image building. Businesses usually employ image advertising to establish an identity or to correct some erroneous view about themselves. Large diversified corporations use it to simplify and clarify their public image.

Although the results achieved by corporate programs are uncertain, there's no uncertainty about their considerable expense. U.S. companies with programs spent an average of more than $1.5 million each in 1980.

Who's using corporate programs?

The larger the company, the more apt it is to be a corporate advertiser (see *Exhibit I*). While 81% of the top *Fortune* "100" industrials use such campaigns, only 26% of the companies ranked "401" through "500" do. Larger companies, individually and collectively, spend more as well. Corporations in the top 20% spend about 78% of what is spent by *Fortune* "500" companies on such programs annually. On average over a period of years, two-thirds of the *Fortune* "250" nonindustrial companies used corporate advertising, with the top half spending 85% of the dollars spent.

Of course, larger companies may have more cash available or may be more willing to take advantage of all the business tools at their disposal. However, research indicates that it is not size per se but conditions related to size that cause the largest companies to pursue corporate campaigns. The larger a company, the greater its complexity, diversity, extent of product line, number of businesses, and geographic dispersion.

A recent cartoon depicted a business executive saying, "Frankly we've diversified so much lately, I'm not sure what business I'm in." Thus, larger companies more often feel a need to use advertising that provides a simple image—easy to grasp and easily conveyed—to unify their disparate activities.

Relationship to an industry

As *Exhibit II* shows, the percentage of companies within each industry that use corporate advertising is more or less uniform. Nevertheless, certain industries employ it more frequently than others. Many companies, of course, use corporate advertising to address social and environmental concerns. The top 20 companies in the oil industry are all corporate campaigners, in large part because of frequent public criticism of their activities. Mobil, in particular, has used such advertising to defend itself against charges of excess profits and lack of interest in environmental protection. And almost all of the largest paper companies have a long-standing tradition of corporate advertising to address environmental issues.

Industrial companies are far more likely to use corporate advertising than are consumer-product companies. For example, 75% of companies in the aerospace industry use it, but only 28% in the food industry.

Packaged goods companies, which spend far more in total advertising dollars than any other industry, spend much less on advertising that addresses their corporate interests. These companies may feel they are already advertising their products enough to establish a necessary presence. More likely they are concerned with spending promotion dollars on what they know best—namely, sales advertising (which brings tangible dollar results). Moreover, my experience shows that the effect of corporate advertising on lower-priced consumer products such as packaged goods is minimal compared with its effect on higher-priced purchases that consumers deliberate more about.

Some packaged goods companies recognize that the image portrayed through a product line may be inappropriate or at odds with what its executives and directors believe to be the true nature of the corporation. Both Philip Morris and the Liggett Group, for example, concluded that their images have been tarnished by the sale of cigarettes. So they now offer "corrective" corporate programs showing some of their other products and interests.

The Liggett Group does this with ads featuring their long line of consumer products, such as Mountain Dew, dog food, and various liquor brands. The copy extols Liggett's diversification and future as a

Exhibit I

Corporate advertising by company size, 1979
in $ thousands

			Number of companies	Number of corporate advertisers	Percent of corporate advertisers	Average corporate ad budget	Corporate ads as percentage of total ads
Fortune "500" industrials		1-50	50	47	94 %	$ 5,210	8 %
		51-100	50	34	68 %	$ 1,971	4 %
		101-200	100	58	58 %	$ 965	2 %
		201-300	100	44	44 %	$ 418	2 %
		301-400	100	35	35 %	$ 243	4 %
		401-500	100	26	26 %	$ 238	6 %
		Total	**500**	**244**	**49 %**	**$ 1,643**	**5 %**
Fortune "250" nonindustrials	Banking	1-25	25	19	76 %	$ 2,071	31 %
		26-50	25	9	36 %	$ 752	40 %
	Life insurance	1-25	25	16	64 %	$ 1,482	60 %
		26-50	25	12	48 %	$ 203	22 %
	Utilities	1-25	25	14	56 %	$ 2,573	33 %
		26-50	25	9	36 %	$ 632	52 %
	Transportation	1-25	25	15	60 %	$ 885	6 %
		26-50	25	2	8 %	$ 126	19 %
	Diversified financial	1-25	25	15	60 %	$ 1,717	15 %
		26-50	25	9	36 %	$ 1,265	45 %

Exhibit II

Corporate advertising by industry, 1979
in $ thousands

		Number of companies	Number of corporate advertisers	Percent of corporate advertisers	Average corporate ad budget	Corporate ads as percentage of total ads
Fortune "500" industrials	Aerospace	12	9	75 %	$ 1,348	29 %
	Chemicals	39	17	44 %	$ 972	5 %
	Electronics-appliances	34	20	59 %	$ 2,849	8 %
	Food	54	15	28 %	$ 551	1 %
	Industrial & farm equipment	44	25	57 %	$ 629	7 %
	Metals manufacturing	41	24	59 %	$ 1,387	51 %
	Mining & crude oil production	12	7	58 %	$ 243	57 %
	Motor vehicles	21	12	57 %	$ 4,725	10 %
	Office equipment	12	6	50 %	$ 5,495	55 %
	Paper, fiber & wood products	30	18	60 %	$ 1,517	22 %
	Petroleum refining	36	21	58 %	$ 4,978	29 %
	Pharmaceuticals	17	10	59 %	$ 83	less than 1%
	Rubber	7	5	71 %	$ 1,716	4 %
	All others	148	55	37 %	$ 461	1 %
	Total	**500**	**244**	**49 %**	**$ 1,643**	**5 %**
Fortune "250" nonindustrials	Banking	50	28	56 %	$ 1,647	32 %
	Life insurance	50	28	56 %	$ 934	52 %
	Utilities	50	23	46 %	$ 1,813	35 %
	Transportation	50	17	34 %	$ 840	6 %
	Diversified financial	50	24	48 %	$ 1,548	19 %

growth company. Philip Morris's approach is less direct; its ads trumpet the company's sponsorship of art as well as the areas of the world in which it has business interests.

Other twists

Some corporations deliberately dissociate themselves from their brand names to protect their reputations against product failure. Other companies find themselves with acquired brand names whose consumer advertising is of little benefit to the corporate identity. Many campaigns (such as those by GTE, TRW, and ITT) are designed to fill this void. GTE's ads present the company's technological achievements in telecommunications as surprising innovations. This leads to the response "Gee! No, GTE" and creates a link that (1) ensures association of the corporate name with innovation and (2)works to eliminate the memory block inherent in perception of an acronym.

A number of companies use an image campaign as an umbrella over many products – Kraft (now a part of Dart & Kraft) is one. While some may call this corporate advertising, the approach also has sales objectives. Corporate campaigns may also substitute for product advertising when there are long lines of products or systems.

What can the corporate campaign accomplish?

Under the right conditions corporate ads can help accomplish many of the following objectives:

...boost sales

The relationship between corporate advertising and sales appears to vary by product class. For example, the effect on the sale of frequently purchased packaged goods is less than on high-priced industrial goods. Similarly, simple low-technology products probably will not benefit from corporate ad programs to the extent that high-technology items will. In high-tech, customers place a great deal of importance on the reputation and expertise of the manufacturer.

...hold employees

Sometimes corporate advertising can improve employee morale significantly. Advertising that imparts a better understanding of where the cor-

poration is going, what it's doing in other parts of the world, and what career opportunities it offers may impress employees. Moreover, many people feel good about themselves if they find that the company where they work is known and respected.

Putting a dollar figure on the savings attained by reducing employee turnover is difficult. Some say you should add recruitment and training costs, next multiply by the turnover rate, and then estimate the percentage of employees who might be persuaded to stay if they felt more positively about the company. Whatever the real figure, if corporate advertising can effect even a modest reduction in turnover, the saving to a large corporation is well worth the expense and effort of a campaign.

...recruit professionals

Corporate advertising helps recruitment – particularly in high-technology industries, where competition for scientists, engineers, and geophysicists is intense. The most desirable graduates are apt to go to companies that supposedly are most progressive and offer the best career opportunities. Such companies as Motorola, National Semiconductor, Exxon Office Systems, and AT&T conduct corporate-recruitment ad programs that supplement job advertisements.

A search for geologists (in great demand in the petroleum industry) sparked Union Texas Petroleum's recent corporate ad campaign. Some companies in the electronics field also used this approach to compete for top students and scientists. GTE's corporate ad program is in part designed to showcase the exciting scientific aspects of the company and to offset the staid public-telephone portion of their operations.

...increase the price of your stock

A corporation with millions of outstanding shares can benefit substantially from a small but lasting improvement in its stock price. Although stock analysts may not learn much that's new about a company from corporate advertising, they may be impressed by numerous inquiries about a company's stock and may go on to study it in more detail. Advertisements can indeed trigger inquiries from potential investors.

One of the few pieces of concrete evidence of a link between corporate advertising and stock price comes from W.R. Grace's 1980 television advertising campaign, their "Look into Grace" series. The commercials highlighted the company's excellent business and financial attributes and then asked "Shouldn't you look into Grace?" After the commercials ran for 13 weeks in test markets, conventional studies of attitude and awareness indicated that familiarity and approval were at significantly higher levels than before the campaign.

When the campaign began, Grace's management believed that the company stock was significantly undervalued. During the 13-week test, its stock's price increased dramatically. Later campaigns, however, did not drive the price any higher. Steve Elliott, corporate ad director of W.R. Grace, notes: "Starting from a very undervalued situation, we reached what seemed to be an appropriate point for the price—much as a product may be priced up to a given point but no further."

I interpret the relationship between corporate campaigns and stock pricing this way: advertising cannot drive up the price of a reasonably priced stock and, indeed, doing so might not be entirely legal; it can, however, work to ensure that a company's shares are not overlooked or undervalued.

Two Northwestern University professors, Eugene Schoenfeld and John Boyd, made an ambitious, though controversial, attempt to go beyond case histories in proving a relationship between corporate advertising and stock prices. They performed a large-scale econometric analysis of the link. Corporate campaigns, they found, have a statistically significant, positive impact on stock prices. By examining the stock performance of 731 companies with sales in excess of $200 million in 1971, 1972, and 1973—and by allowing for the normal independent variables—they determined that such advertising's positive influence averages about 2%. The influence was greatest when the stock market was moving up but not noticeable when the market was heading down.

Of course, advertising can't project a false image for long without crippling the advertiser. If financial factors are wreaking havoc on your stock prices, make sure you really want your story communicated to the financial community. Gaining the attention of investors and analysts when your company's financial structure is shaky would be less than prudent.

After studying others' results, I succumbed to the temptation to compare the performances of corporate advertisers with nonadvertisers. Although I realized that no cause and effect would be demonstrated, I thought it would be interesting to see if corporate advertisers were indeed more profitable companies. For the record, I could find no difference in profitability or profit improvement among campaigners and nonbelievers. On reflection, I concluded that such results are entirely appropriate: corporate programs are rarely directed primarily at increasing profitability.

...get people to understand you

More attention has been focused on advocacy advertising than its limited use should warrant. My research reveals that less than 5% of corporate advertising expenditures go toward such issue advertising. This may be due to reticence on the part of some companies to characterize their messages this way; but even if this figure were doubled, it would still represent only a minor part of corporate advertising. (A few respondents did indicate that issue advertising constitutes almost 100% of their activity.)

My findings correlate with the Association of National Advertisers' 1979 corporate advertising survey.[1] Only 14 of the 173 corporate advertisers who responded to that questionnaire listed their program's primary objective as getting people to react in one way or another to some issue. However, 19% of the respondents did include such a goal among their aims, and 22% of the respondents listed as one of their goals a somewhat similar objective ("to communicate the company's concern and record of achievement on social or environmental issues").

While fewer than a fifth of advertisers consider swaying public opinion an objective, all companies do in fact seek social support and understanding. If there is one objective common to every corporate program it is to be better understood as a corporation—whether by financial analysts, prospective employees, current employees, the government, or regulatory bodies. Management hopes, of course, that this better understanding will spur supportive behavior from its various publics. Such behavior might entail buying or recommending its stock, favoring its offerings, deciding to purchase its products, siding with it if a controversy arises, or recommending the company as a place to work.

Although many companies assume that the safest course is to keep a low profile, this may in fact be a dangerous tack. If some inadvertent disclosure brings high visibility or even incidental exposure, an unknown company maintains little credibility as it moves to counter public criticism. The almost unknown Hooker Chemical Company became infamous within a matter of weeks. It was unprepared to present its side of the Love Canal story convincingly. On the other hand, a widely known company, Richardson Merrell, maintained a credible image throughout the horrendous thalidomide disaster.

When people first get acquainted with a company through an unfortunate disclosure, they often distort what little they know and make generalizations about missing information. The less filled out a company's image is, the more subject that image is to wild distortions. It is important to give the people whose good opinion business depends on a complete view of a corporation and its positive role in society, not just through corporate advertising but through all channels of corporate communications.

1 Association of National Advertisers, Inc. survey report, "Current Company Practices in the Use of Corporate Advertising."

How the study was done

In January 1981, I sent questionnaires and accompanying letters to the chief executive officers of the *Fortune* "500" industrial companies and the "300" *Fortune* nonindustrial companies. Because I did not use the responses from retailers, the number of nonindustrials studied was reduced to 250. I had a response rate of 44% from the industrial companies and a 42% rate from the nonindustrial businesses.

Of the 221 industrial companies that responded, 102 indicated that they do practice corporate advertising, 82 said they do not, and 37 didn't answer the question. Among these 221 respondents, 139 reported that they engage in general advertising, 17 do not, and 65 did not answer that question.

None of the 7 retailers who answered the question about corporate advertising reported any expenditures for it, so I removed the 11 responses from retailers. Of the 116 non-retailers in nonindustrial businesses, 73 said they are corporate advertisers, 36 indicated that they are not, and 7 did not reply. Eighty-five of these 116 respondents do advertise, 16 don't at all, and 15 didn't answer the question about total advertising.

Criteria for the decision

So should you or shouldn't you use corporate advertising in your company? You should certainly consider it if your company's stock seems to be significantly undervalued or if you are in an industry that carries a higher than usual risk of unwanted publicity.

For many companies, however, the decision to engage in such advertising is not so clear-cut. In such cases, I suggest that top managers do the following:

1   Assign the task of evaluating the possible benefits from a corporate campaign to the corporate communications director. (Such advertising should be well integrated with corporate public relations activities; normally, it should not be assigned to the advertising function as that function exists in the marketing hierarchy.)

2   Encourage the CEO to work closely with the corporate communications director, sharing the five-year plans for the corporation and determining how the company is to be publicly portrayed. This portrait should be condensed into a short statement of corporate mission.

3   Authorize research to analyze the public's attitudes toward and level of awareness of the company, concentrating on people important to the business.

4   Include in-house investor-relations groups from the beginning. Also invite other managers to participate closely in designing the campaigns, because they may have already conducted relevant research.

5   If research suggests that people view your corporation differently from the way you'd like them to, add corporate advertising to your total communications mix. However, if the difference between the image you would like and the one you actually have is based on real shortcomings in the corporation's performance or structure, you should correct these problems first. A flattering picture painted with deceptive information will eventually be discovered and denounced.

6   Call on consultants if necessary. If you are already allied with a reputable agency with proven corporate advertising skills, turn there for assistance.

7   Finally, if you do develop a program, ensure that the CEO continues to be involved. One or more subsidiaries may have strong ad departments, but the corporate communications director's staff should handle corporate advertising – with a short line to the top. ▽

Reprint 82204

Comparative
Advertising

Us vs. Them: The Minefield of Comparative Ads

Make sure you won't be liable for a lawsuit by a competitor charging that you've made a false claim.

by Bruce Buchanan and Doron Goldman

To introduce its more effective eye drops, Schering-Plough took aim at the market leader with this line in its magazine ads: "New OcuClear relieves three times longer than Visine." To tout its exclusive manufacturing process that makes Folgers decaffeinated crystals produce darker coffee, Procter & Gamble ran print ads with Folgers and "the leading brand" (Sanka) prepared in see-through glass cups. The copy read, "Looks so dark and rich, shouldn't you switch?" To establish the superiority of its household cleaner, Bristol-Myers ran TV commercials claiming, "New Liquid Vanish really does clean tough rust stains below the water line better than Lysol," and showing the two brands in action.

As these cases show, comparative advertising is a hard-bitten, attention-grabbing way of saying, "We're better than the competition." Time was when good manners and (perhaps) fear of retaliation limited derogatory comparisons to Our Brand vs. Brand X, but today few advertis-

ers are so timid or so cautious as to mask the identity of the competition when contrasting aspects of their own goods against those of the other big player or players in the market.

A comparative ad campaign can, however, land you in a lawsuit in federal court. The disparaged rival may sue you, claiming that you have distorted the facts or even invented them. The suit and the resulting publicity may call into question not only the quality of your research but also the integrity of your product and even the reputation of your company. If you lose the litigation, a retraction and payment of damages could be very painful.

The issue of comparative advertising has taken on new life since last November, when President Reagan signed trademark legislation making it easier to sue competitors for advertising attacks. According to the Trademark Law Revision Act of 1988, anyone is vulnerable to a civil action who "misrepresents the nature, characteristics, qualities, or geo-

graphical origin of his or her or another person's goods, services, or commercial activities." The wording closes a loophole in the Lanham Act, which had governed this advertising tactic for 43 years. Lanham had made no mention of "another person's" goods; it had prohibited only false claims about one's own goods.

It's too early to tell, of course, whether the toughened law will provoke a rash of lawsuits alleging injury from competitors' misrepresentations. But there has been no shortage of such actions under the Lanham Act: we have counted more than 60 published judicial opinions in comparative ad cases, 30 of them since 1985 after this type of assault had become widespread. Even this number is conservative, since many more cases were doubtless resolved before a verdict or did not result in issuance of a judicial opinion.

Obviously, not all such ads spawn lawsuits, or are even contested. Even when they are contested, many are resolved at the TV networks or at the National Advertising Division of the Council of Better Business Bureaus, where an aggrieved marketer can also bring a challenge. But our research shows that many companies have elected to take rivals to court under the Lanham Act because of the broad information-discovery powers under the federal civil procedure rules, the speed with which a competitor can stop the offending ad campaign through a preliminary injunction, and the possibility of collecting damages.

Therefore, every comparative advertiser should be ready to go to court. Once your competitor files suit, you can do little to stop the process. Early preparation will yield better returns when the papers are

Bruce Buchanan is an associate professor of marketing at the Stern School of Business, New York University, where he specializes in marketing research. An expert on comparative advertising, he also wrote for HBR on the subject in 1985. Doron Goldman returned to academia from the practice of law to pursue a doctorate in marketing at New York University.

served. To be prepared, you have to know what the federal courts will allow and use this knowledge in devising your advertising. (Moreover, your company may be headquartered in a state that has a law prohibiting defamation and disparagement in comparative advertising cases. So you may have to be doubly prepared.)

We have surveyed the federal court record and determined the conditions under which your comparative ad is likely to stand and, more important, the flaws that would cause it to be enjoined in court. We aim to make it very difficult for your competitor to demonstrate that your messages have any of these flaws. Of course, no single article can lay out an exhaustive reference on this topic; but if you follow the principles here, your advertising will be much less vulnerable to challenge.

> ## You have to know what the federal courts will allow, and devise your ads accordingly.

Fidelity matters

A comparative claim is usually based on two types of data. First, there are facts. If you claim to have more flights to Chicago than your competitor, you have made a factual statement that can be verified or refuted with certainty.

Second, there are research results. If you claim that your digestive aid makes people "feel better faster," the basis for your claim will usually be a set of research data, the outcome of some scientific procedure. Here the truth or falsity of the assertion depends on the procedure used. Did you have the right people in the study? Did they use the aids as instructed? Were there any conditions that may have biased the results? These are questions on which different qualified researchers often have different opinions, so there is no way to answer them once and for all. Nevertheless, many comparative claims are based on research results, and the manager must know the pitfalls of using them.

The claim is often set before the supporting research is conducted. From prior studies and in-house knowledge, you may believe that your antiperspirant "stops wetness longer." So you commission a study by an independent research supplier to compare your brand with a competitor's—fully expecting to corroborate your belief. Such prudence allows the company to support a statement with more expensive research designed to meet higher standards than it would normally meet. Subjects are selected more carefully, for example, and a more valid protocol is used. Most important, the study is designed to collect *all* those data and *only* those data pertaining to the claim.

The marketer decides what the claim will be, guides the researcher in collecting data, and works with agency people to translate the claim into the words and pictures of the advertisement. The company has one primary responsibility here: to ensure that the ad reflects the supporting data with fidelity. By this we mean that the message must correctly and completely communicate the underlying data to the audience without distortion or omission, just as pictures and sound are communicated with fidelity from a television station to your set. Any material infidelity in the ad will almost surely result in its injunction.

Because corporate executives form the connection between researcher and copywriter and because they bear responsibility for the success of the ad, they must make sure that fidelity is achieved. Only they are in a position to do this.

Federal law does not *require* ad substantiation; it *prohibits* falsity. As defendant, the advertiser is under no obligation to prove the claim to be true; rather, the competitor as plaintiff must prove it false. Consequently, in Lanham Act cases, courts have rarely enjoined ads for inadequate substantiation.

Virtually all injunctions in these cases have been obtained because the plaintiff showed either that (1) the words and pictures in the ad did not fully and accurately reflect the supporting data or other known facts or (2) the ad, though literally true, misled consumers into believing something false about the product. Nearly always, judges issue comparative ad injunctions after the plaintiff has

DRAWING BY PAUL MEISEL

shown an infidelity in the way the ad communicates the data. For this reason, fidelity matters.

A competitor has grounds to sue, by the way, even if its brand is not

Federal law doesn't require substantiation of a claim; it does prohibit falsity.

named in an ad. Alberto-Culver took action against Gillette regarding a hair rinse commercial. Gillette contended that the allegation did not fall under the Lanham Act because the commercial said nothing about Alberto-Culver's product. The court held, however, that the law gives competitors a cause of action for false statements an advertiser makes about its own product "alone or in comparison with the goods of a competitor."[1] Thus any competitor "likely to be damaged" by a comparative ad can bring suit; it need not be named in the ad. On a practical level, this means that general superiority claims like "most preferred taste" or "lowest gas consumption" can be challenged by unnamed competitors.

Infidelity checklist

Here is a list of infidelities. Each has killed at least one comparative advertisement. In each case, the company could have saved itself much trouble and expense by following these guidelines.

Don't contradict the facts. This may not sound profound, but it's very important. At 2 milligrams per cigarette, Now once claimed to have the "lowest 'tar' of all cigarettes." But another brand in the market, Carlton 70, had only 1 milligram. Even though Now was a king-size brand and Carlton 70 was shorter, the claim said "all cigarettes," so it contradicted a known fact. Not surprisingly, the court enjoined it.[2]

Don't contradict the research results. Sometimes an advertiser constructs a claim that belies its own research results. E.P.T. Plus, a home pregnancy test, allegedly gave results

in "as soon as 10 minutes." Tambrands, a competitor, brought suit, saying that the statement was false. To support its position, Warner-Lambert, the maker of E.P.T. Plus, produced the results of a study of 19 pregnant women. Of these, 10 obtained positive (that is, pregnant) test results within 10 minutes; 2 obtained positive results within 30 minutes; the remaining 7 obtained false negative results. Warner-Lambert argued that the claim was true because "the overwhelming majority of women...will in fact obtain accurate results in 10 minutes, even on Day 1."

But the court decided that the data did not support the claim because "48% of the pregnant women in the study did not receive accurate test results in 10 minutes." Other results showed that the test usually took 30 minutes to return a negative result, and the court noted that "more than half of the women who purchase kits want to know that they are not pregnant." Because the assertion contradicted Warner-Lambert's own research, the judge enjoined it.[3]

Had Tambrands relied on conflicting research results, the court would have had to determine whether they invalidated the advertiser's. This is a murky area, and courts are reluctant to decide these matters. But because Warner-Lambert's *own* results contradicted the claim, the court did not have to make any such decision. The advertiser had committed an infidelity.

Don't overstep your data. Do not make unqualified claims based on qualified results. Castrol GTX motor oil's ad said that an "independent lab test reveals that, unlike Quaker State, Castrol does not lose viscosity." There are, however, two types of viscosity loss: temporary, where the molecules of the oil additives bend under the stress of engine operation but recover their original shapes when the engine stops running; and permanent, where the molecules break and cannot recover. Quaker State Oil Refining Corporation brought suit against Burmah-Castrol, Inc.

Testimony revealed that all motor oils, Castrol included, suffer some

temporary loss of viscosity, and the data on which Burmah-Castrol based the claim measured only permanent viscosity loss. The court found that the claim "may be fairly read to mean that Castrol never loses viscosity even temporarily in an operating engine" and that it was "literally false." Quaker State won an injunction stopping the ad.[4]

Similarly, Westwood Lighting's new process for finishing lamps purportedly provided "superior quality control, superior manufacturing technology, a superior lighting product." The court found, however, that the results Westwood presented in support of its claim "did not address ...the quality control, the manufacturing technology, or, finally, the total lighting product," but focused

Don't stretch qualified research results to make unqualified claims.

only on the durability of the lacquer finish on the lamps. Westwood had taken specific research results and embellished them to come up with a general superiority claim. The court found it to be "patently false" and enjoined it.[5]

Everyone wants a broad, strong claim, but you have to resist the temptation to remove the qualifiers. Someone has to rein in the copywriters. It's worth noting that Westwood Lighting's CEO reviewed the supporting research before approving the claim. Even so, the execution overstepped the data.

Don't cherry-pick the results. A research study may furnish some results that favor your brand and some that don't. You may be sorely tempted to use only the favorable data as a basis for your message, but hold on! You cannot just ask a number of questions on a consumer survey and cherry-pick the ones that favor your brand.

To support a claim against Winston Lights, Triumph cigarettes conducted a consumer survey that asked four major questions. On two of these (pertaining to "preference" and "better" taste), Triumph won a majority of votes, but on the other two (pertaining to "amount of taste" and "satisfying quality"), it did not. Triumph based its advertising claim on the results of the first two questions and largely ignored the others. R.J. Reynolds, manufacturer of Winstons, sued Loews Theaters, producers of Triumphs.

The court found that Triumph had "failed to establish a basis" on which to disregard the results of the last two questions, since these also asked about the relative quality of the two brands. It also held that "failure to disclose a material aspect of the results, relating to taste, under the circumstances is misleading."[6] The lesson is clear: if you commission a survey in support of a comparative claim, collect only those data that pertain to the claim and are likely to support it.

But the dangers of selective reporting extend beyond claims based on consumer surveys. Johnson & Johnson distributed to doctors a "safety profile" of Tylenol. It listed three over-the-counter analgesics – Tylenol, plain/buffered aspirin, and Ibuprofen – with a checklist of 17 side effects. Tylenol had fewer side effects than the others. The checklist did not, however, mention potential liver damage or danger from overdoses, where Tylenol presents greater risks than the other drugs. In other words, the checklist omitted those characteristics that put Tylenol at a disadvantage.

Johnson & Johnson's lawyers argued that it was under no obligation to report these because the Lanham Act is not a "full-disclosure law." But the court held that concealing the disadvantages of the drug "creates an unacceptable potential for misleading even the professional audience at which it was directed."[7] Thus, where the health of consumers is involved, there is an even greater imperative to avoid cherry-picking.

Don't use the truth to mislead. Even a claim that is literally true may be enjoined under federal law if it is found to be misleading. The federal courts have held that "the

Lanham Act encompasses more than literal falsehoods....Were it otherwise, clever use of innuendo, indirect intimations, and ambiguous suggestions could shield the advertisement from scrutiny precisely when protection against such sophisticated deception is most needed."[8]

But the plaintiff cannot merely assert that the ad is misleading. In the case we cited concerning Now cigarettes, R.J. Reynolds did modify its claim to read "Now. 2mg 'tar' is the lowest (king size or longer)." The parenthetic text qualifies the claim to allow for Carlton 70, but the Carlton king-size brands also contained 2 milligrams of tar. Is this claim false with respect to Carlton kings? Literally, no. It says that 2 milligrams of tar is the lowest level in king-size cigarettes, which is true, and it does not say that Now is the only brand at this level. Still, a casual reading might lead consumers to conclude erroneously that it was.

American Brands asserted that this claim was misleading, but the court did not find in its favor because the company introduced no "evidence of substance" to demonstrate that consumers were being misled. Thus a court can enjoin a claim that contradicts, embellishes, or cherry-picks. But to obtain an injunction against a claim that is literally true, the plaintiff must prove, by a preponderance of the evidence, that it is misleading.

The plaintiff can usually obtain this proof by means of an ad communication test. Here consumers view an ad and report the message it conveys to them. If enough consumers report an incorrect message, the ad is judged to be misleading.

In the never-ending analgesic wars, American Home Products once made the claim, "For pain other than headache, Anacin reduces the inflammation that comes with the pain. These [Tylenol, Datril] do not." Johnson & Johnson contended in court that this claim was in fact a general superiority claim and therefore false, while AHP maintained that the assertion referred merely to inflammation reduction. J&J, however, submitted the results of a test showing that 31% of those who

had viewed the ad reported a "general message of superiority" that was not qualified by the anti-inflammatory copy.

Basing this judgment on this and other communication tests, the judge ruled that "the preponderance of the evidence supports the claim that the commercial made a broad representation that Anacin gives su-

> **A court can enjoin a claim that contradicts, embellishes, or cherry-picks.**

perior pain relief." And since the court also found that the two brands were equally effective as general analgesics, it enjoined the commercial.[9]

What proportion of consumers must be misled to justify enjoining? That's a good question that has no good answer. Each case is decided in context. In a case involving a Tropicana orange juice TV commercial, a communication test showed "a level of consumer confusion significantly below 15%," and the lower court ruled that this was insufficient for a preliminary injunction.[10] This seems reasonable because more than 85% of consumers were not confused. (Most advertisers would be thrilled to get their message across to 85% of viewers.)

But the plaintiff, Coca-Cola, appealed, and a higher court reversed the decision. The appeals court held that when "a not insubstantial number of consumers" is misled, there is "sufficient evidence of risk of irreparable harm" to warrant injunction.[11] Recently, however, a court decided in another case that "the pertinent issue is not the specific percentage of deception revealed in the survey, but rather the tendency to deceive."[12]

Now, the terms "not insubstantial" and "tendency to deceive" are open to interpretation; clearly the federal judiciary is choosing not to set a threshold that separates a misleading claim from one that isn't.

Still, these opinions do indicate that even a mildly misleading claim may be enjoined. Truth in comparative advertising is not enough; you must also be clear.

Never set out to make a false or misleading claim. If a court finds such intent, it will assume that you "accomplished" your purpose and enjoin the ad. Again, the analgesic wars illustrate the point. Maximum Strength Anacin, with 500 milligrams of aspirin, was positioned as a uniquely strong pain reliever—indeed, among aspirin-based products, the strongest formulation. And the ad copy did qualify the claim by saying it was the strongest "in the pain reliever doctors recommend most"—aspirin. But McNeilab, the Johnson & Johnson subsidiary that makes Extra Strength Tylenol (a non-aspirin formula also containing 500 milligrams of pain reliever), contended in a lawsuit against American Home Products that the commercial falsely claimed that Maximum Strength Anacin was the strongest formula for *any* over-the-counter analgesic.

This contention could have been decided using the results of a communication test, but McNeilab introduced evidence showing that AHP management knew of the commercial's potential to mislead. Both its own research staff and the broadcast standards department of a television network had raised questions about it. Yet AHP persisted in airing the ad. The court concluded that the company knew of its potential to mislead and cited this knowledge in enjoining the claim.[13]

In a number of advertisements, Jartran claimed it could "save the consumer big money to almost any city on truck and trailer rentals" compared with U-Haul. A federal court found this claim to be false, deceptive, and misleading. Jartran was promoting special introductory prices as if they were permanent. But more important, Jartran had intended to deceive the consumer. The company had created pictures for its ads showing its trucks and U-Hauls "with the comparative sizes of the vehicles adjusted to make the U-Haul truck appear smaller and less attractive." Denouncing the ads as "deliberately false," the court enjoined them.[14]

When Jartran appealed the decision, the circuit court reinforced the finding that the intention to deceive creates the presumption that deception actually occurred. So if your competitor can show that you set out to deceive or mislead, you will bear the burden of proving that you did not. This is important: in such situations, contrary to all others we have discussed, the burden of proof shifts from the plaintiff to the defendant. In the court's words, "He who has attempted to deceive should not complain when required to bear the burden of rebutting a presumption that he succeeded."[15] Thus bad intentions cost you the presumption of innocence.

Pictures count too. False pictures can get your ad enjoined just as false words can. The Tropicana Premium Pack orange juice TV commercial mentioned earlier showed Olympic athlete Bruce Jenner squeezing juice from an orange and pouring it into a Tropicana carton, saying, "It's pure pasteurized juice as it comes from the orange." The message was that Tropicana, unlike other leading brands, was not made from concentrate. Coca-Cola, which produces rival Minute Maid, sued.

The court found this visual sequence to be false because Tropicana juice was not squeezed from the orange directly into cartons, as the commercial depicted; it was pasteurized and sometimes frozen first. The court also said that Jenner's qualifying voice-over was insufficient because "pasteurized juice does not come from oranges." The judge granted an injunction.

Though it may escape the charge of falsity, a picture can make an ad misleading. An Advil television commercial showed a sequence in which a Tylenol pill rolled away and was replaced by an Advil pill. The ad stated that Advil was "like Tylenol," which is a parity claim. Once more Johnson & Johnson and American Home Products squared off in litigation.

*"They all work on the floor of the stock exchange and
it takes them a while to unwind."*

Considering the results of consumer communication tests, the court ruled the overall impression to be "that Advil represents the current state of the art, a definite advance over Tylenol." The picture created a misleading impression by turning a parity claim into a superiority claim. The judge enjoined the ad.[16]

But don't the data matter?

So far we have discussed the connection between the data and the message. But particularly in the case of research results, the marketer should ask: Do the data accurately measure what they purport to measure? Have we used the right methodology? Have we surveyed the right people? These questions of validity naturally are a central concern for researchers. The courts, however, tend to hold back on making judgments about the quality of the data used to support a claim. This follows from the fact that the Lanham Act, while prohibiting false representations, says nothing about substantiation or the lack thereof. Still, our research into the court record has uncovered some useful insights in this area.

When plaintiff and defendant present conflicting data to support opposing claims, the court will not necessarily deem one claim to be true and the other false. Chesebrough-Pond's and Procter & Gamble sued each other because the claims of their skin treatments ("no leading lotion beats" Vaseline Intensive Care and "New Wondra relieves dry skin better than any other leading lotion") were contradictory. Both advertisers marshaled clinical data to support their assertions and each tried to discredit the other's data. But after analysis in which it found that both sets of data were of dubious quality, the court held that neither party had shown by "a preponderance of the evidence" that the other's claim was false. Therefore, neither party was entitled to injunctive relief, and both claims were allowed to stand unchanged.[17]

Furthermore, judges tend to reason in terms of fidelity even when the data betray problems. The E.P.T. Plus claim got substantiation from the merest majority (10) of a sample of 19 women. Any researcher reviewing these data would immediately ask:
■ How were these 19 women chosen for the study? Answer: They were enrolled at a Cincinnati fertility clinic, so they weren't exactly a random sample of the target market.
■ Is your "overwhelming majority" statistically significant? Answer: No. For a 52% majority to be significantly more than half, you need a sample of about 1,700 women.

But the court said only that the "questionable statistical validity of the study is not important because the results...do not support defendant's claims." Finding infidelity between the data and the claim, the judge saw no need to decide on the quality of the data.

Finally, the burden of discrediting data lies with the plaintiff. An Abbott Labs advertisement for Tronolane made a preference statement against Preparation H based on a questionable survey. (In the survey, Tronolane was identified as a test product, and it is known that, as the court later put it, respondents tend to "please the tester by preferring the test product.") American Home Products raised this issue in federal court in behalf of its product, Preparation H, but it had no data that showed the claim to be false.

While noting the problem, the court held that it would "require substantial proof of invalidity before enjoining the results of any test that is colorably valid." Furthermore, the court decided it would be undesirable to enjoin ads "solely on the basis of a theoretical challenge to the test methodology."[18] Thus a plaintiff can get an injunction by reason of false data only by showing that a better data collection method exists and that, when it is used, it invalidates the claim.

R.J. Reynolds took this approach in challenging the Triumph ad that we discussed before. In the Triumph preference survey, the brand names were not divulged, but respondents were told which cigarette had 3 milligrams of tar and which had 14 milligrams, and told that they should consider this difference in making their choices. The 66% of the votes that Triumph got, to Winston Lights'

29%, became the basis of the claim. RJR replicated the survey, without disclosing the tar content, and Winston Lights won 54% to 40%.

Thus RJR showed that the Triumph survey did not measure taste preference, as it purported to, but taste and tar preference. Furthermore, RJR demonstrated that the taste preference claim was false when the more valid methodology was employed. "The test was therefore deceptive," the court concluded, "and the advertising based upon it reflected that quality."

This is the only case we have found, however, where the plaintiff demonstrated falsity by discrediting the data. In fact, the judge wrote, "no prior court had enjoined comparative advertising because of the consumer survey methodology underlying the ad." So this approach, not generally supported by case law, requires the plaintiff to come to court prepared with its own evidence.

When the papers are served

Your first inkling of a challenge to your advertising will come when a competitor files in federal court for a preliminary injunction. A hearing can take place in a week or two after filing, and if the plaintiff prevails, the judge will enjoin your ad from that point forward. The court will grant an injunction if your competitor can show probable success on the merits and possible irreparable injury. In other words, the competitor must establish that the claim probably is false or misleading and that the competitor would suffer irreparable harm, such as loss of market share or goodwill, if your allegation were allowed to air until after discovery and a trial.

If the preliminary injunction is denied, your competitor is likely to appeal instead of pursue a trial. The reasons for this are time and money. In the appealed Tropicana case, the higher court reversed the district court's denial in less than five months. A trial, with its requirement of full discovery, would likely have taken more time and cost more.

Moreover, the preliminary injunction standard of "probable success" is very similar to the full-trial determination of "preponderance of the evidence," so it is unlikely that the lower court will find in your competitor's favor in a trial after denying preliminary relief unless the plaintiff introduces substantial new evidence.

You can be sued for damages under federal law, but the plaintiff must demonstrate harm. U-Haul sought damages as well as an injunction against Jartran, and the court found in its favor, awarding $20 million in compensatory damages and another $20 million in punitive damages. U-Haul had a virtual monopoly in the self-move market and it had done no print advertising other than in the Yellow Pages, so it was able to demonstrate damage in lost sales and higher advertising costs. Most advertisers, however, are not monopolists, so it's hard to ascribe the losses of one player in the market to the actions of another.

When you are served with papers, consider a countersuit. Let's return to the analgesic wars: American Home Products sued for a declaratory judgment against Johnson & Johnson, seeking a prohibition against interference with the comparative advertising of AHP's Anacin. J&J, whose subsidiary makes Tylenol, countersued and won an injunction against AHP. Later, in behalf of Anacin and Advil, AHP won an injunction against certain Tylenol claims, but J&J countersued and won an injunction barring certain practices connected with Anacin and Advil advertising. The best defense may indeed be a good offense. Another good offensive tactic is your own ad campaign that refutes or negates your opponent's.

Another consideration is the cost of doing battle under federal law. The litigation and research required to defend a comparative ad claim can be painfully expensive and wasteful. Federal Judge William C. Conner, reviewing the ten-year court battle among the analgesic brands, wrote ruefully, "Small nations have fought for their very survival with less resources." When you are trying to manage a business, litigation is both a distraction and a drain on your energies.

Then there is the negative publicity you can get when embarrassing facts become part of the court record. (All the less-than-admirable tactics cited in this article were recorded in published judicial opinions.) You may find that these possible costs outweigh the likely gains.

But if you do decide to run a comparative ad, remember: infidelities are fatal. Make sure your data match your claim. That is especially important now that Uncle Sam has made marketers liable for civil suits for misrepresenting competitors' products.

References

1. Alberto-Culver Company v. The Gillette Company, 408 F. Supp. 1160 (N.D. Ill. Mar. 10, 1976).

2. American Brands, Inc. v. R.J. Reynolds Tobacco Company, 413 F. Supp. 1210 (S.D. N.Y. June 2, 1976).

3. Tambrands v. Warner-Lambert Company, 673 F. Supp. 1190 (S.D. N.Y. June 29, 1987).

4. Quaker State Oil Refining Corporation v. Burmah-Castrol, Inc., 504 F. Supp. 178 (S.D. N.Y. Oct. 17, 1980).

5. Stiffel Company v. Westwood Lighting Group, 658 F. Supp. 1103 (D. N.J. Mar. 19, 1987).

6. R.J. Reynolds Tobacco Company v. Loews Theatres, Inc., 511 F. Supp. 867 (S.D. N.Y. Oct. 24, 1980).

7. American Home Products v. Johnson & Johnson, 654 F. Supp. 568 (S.D. N.Y. Apr. 1, 1987).

8. American Home Products v. Johnson & Johnson, 577 F. 2d 160 (2d Cir. May 1, 1978).

9. American Home Products v. Johnson & Johnson, 436 F. Supp. 785 (S.D. N.Y. Aug. 29, 1977).

10. Coca-Cola Company v. Tropicana Products, Inc., 538 F. Supp. 1091 (S.D. N.Y. May 13, 1982).

11. Coca-Cola Company v. Tropicana Products, Inc., 690 F. 2d 312 (2d Cir. Sept. 29, 1982).

12. Tyco Industries v. Lego Systems, Inc., 5 U.S.P.Q. 2d 1023 (D.N.J. Aug. 26, 1987).

13. McNeilab, Inc. v. American Home Products Corporation, 501 F. Supp. 517 (S.D. N.Y. Nov. 21, 1980).

14. U-Haul International, Inc. v. Jartran, Inc., 601 F. Supp. 1140 (D. Ariz. Nov. 26, 1984).

15. U-Haul International, Inc. v. Jartran, Inc., 793 F. 2d 1034 (9th Cir. July 3, 1986).

16. McNeilab, Inc. v. American Home Products Corporation, 675 F. Supp. 819 (S.D. N.Y. Dec. 1, 1987).

17. Procter & Gamble Company v. Chesebrough-Pond's, Inc., 588 F. Supp. 1082 (S.D. N.Y. June 11, 1984).

18. American Home Products Corporation v. Abbott Laboratories, 522 F. Supp. 1035 (S.D. N.Y. Sept. 18, 1981).

Reprint 89301

"I'm sorry, Mr. Drexler is not available for comment."

Can you pass the comparative ad challenge?

Bruce Buchanan

*Ads that compare products
must be based
on sound research
methods*

We've all seen comparative advertisements. There's "the Pepsi Challenge" that "more people prefer Pepsi to Coke." And the claim that "in shampoo tests...Body on Tap got higher ratings than Prell, Flex, and Sassoon." And the assertion that "Triumph beats Merit!" Such advertisements are blatant in their effort to build up one brand at the expense of another. Less obvious are the data on which the claims are based. While comparative advertisements strongly suggest that rigorous comparative testing has been done, the research may be spotty or weak when analyzed in detail.

The author suggests five essential questions for victims of comparative ads and those contemplating using such ads to ask in evaluating comparative claims. For instance, were consumers actually asked to compare one brand with another? And was the sample of consumers representative of product users? Could subjects really discriminate between the products being compared? Victims who find flaws in the research used to support comparative ads can appeal the findings to various regulatory and judicial authorities and, in some cases, have the offending advertising stopped or changed.

Mr. Buchanan is assistant professor of marketing at New York University, where he specializes in the use of product testing in comparative advertising.

A comparative ad features a sacrificial "victim"—one of the market's leading brands that is made to look inferior to the brand sponsoring the ad. Coca-Cola, for example, has been the victim of "the Pepsi Challenge" and more recently of certain C&C Cola ads. A marketing manager whose brand is victimized in a comparative ad must devise an appropriate response. It can mean doing nothing or appealing to a television network, filing for an injunction or airing a counterclaim. Because the victim's response depends on the quality of the data used to support the comparative claim, an important step in formulating a response is to evaluate the data substantiating the ad.

Comparative ads use either of two types of data: objective data or subjective consumer product test results. Ads based on objective data are usually easy to verify or refute. A good example is the Saab versus Volvo advertisement comparing several features of the two cars, including trunk space, wheel base, and engine size. Anyone can go see if the Saab's rear seat actually folds down; there isn't much room for interpretation.

Comparative ads based on subjective consumer product tests are another matter. These claims are of the form that "more people prefer Brand A to Brand B" or "A is as good as B but costs less." Note Sprite versus 7-Up, Schlitz versus Michelob, Whopper versus Big Mac, Cookin' Good versus Perdue, La Cour Pavillion versus Mouton Cadet, and Diet Pepsi versus Diet Coke, followed by Diet Coke versus Diet Pepsi.

What do "more people prefer" and "is as good as" mean? Probably as many things as there are advertisers. Furthermore, the question formats, the subject selection procedures, the sample sizes, and the choice of language used in reporting test results all in-

Author's note: I wish to thank Donald G. Morrison, Robert Shoemaker, and Subrata Sen for their many helpful comments on this article.

Editor's note: All references appear at the end of the article.

fluence the comparative claims. Consequently, advertisers can misuse product-testing procedures in endless ways.

In this article, I suggest several criteria for evaluating comparative ads. These criteria are based on product-testing technical studies done over the last four years. They are phrased as questions that managers of victimized brands can ask about claims based on a competitor's consumer product test. If the comparative advertiser can answer all the questions satisfactorily, then the claim deserves consideration. If not, the victim may successfully challenge the ad. Of course makers of such ads can use the questions to aid in anticipating possible challenges.

Product testing has been around for a long time, but it has usually been the province of researchers. Because comparative advertising now has serious managerial consequences, all people associated with developing comparative campaigns – brand managers, product-testing experts, and advertising managers – need to know what can and cannot be said about the outcomes of product tests. On the victim's side, the brand manager, the marketing research director, the corporation's lawyers, and even on occasion the chief executive get involved in trying to refute an offensive claim. Many senior managers who have never had anything to do with product testing are finding themselves drawn into the comparative advertising fray.

So this article is addressed to senior managers, who must frequently make decisions about comparative ads. And it is addressed to middle managers, who must formulate the ads and handle associated details.

In my own experience, just two days before the opening of a World Series, lawyers have had to review product test results that ultimately decided the fate of a multimillion-dollar comparative campaign scheduled to begin during the first game. In another case, corporate officials had to review product test procedures for a comparative claim that would be the promotional basis for a new brand rollout. In another situation, a marketing research director for a major soft drink manufacturer took a lot of heat from independent bottlers because their product was repeatedly "getting beaten on TV."

Thus senior managers can no longer afford to leave the issue to research people but must understand the tactics for challenging poorly substantiated comparative ads and weaknesses that often occur in comparative claims.

Managers must also be aware of the opportunities and pitfalls in bringing challenges to the National Advertising Division, the National Advertising Review Board, the Federal Trade Commission, and the courts. The victim's managers must also understand how to obtain the data that support the challenger's claim. For a review of comparative advertising and its implications for the victim, see the insert "The brief history of ads."

Key questions

The brands that use comparative advertising most are those with the least to lose. A manufacturer that has spent years developing a market-leading brand with an image all its own is not going to jeopardize that image by featuring its competitors' products in its ads.

Market leaders try instead to distinguish their brands in the consumer's mind. Coke is not advertised as the best cola; Coke is "The Real Thing" or, more recently, just plain "It." By implication, other colas are "unreal" or maybe "not It," but whatever they are, they are not featured in Coke's ads. Similarly, the producers of Bayer do not merely claim that their brand is better than other aspirin. They state that "only Bayer is 100% pure aspirin" and thus imply that all other aspirins are of some inferior grade not worthy of mention.

The brands with the least to lose are usually those with the smallest market share. These brands have much to gain by featuring a market leader in their ads. They create a brand association that diminishes the special one-of-a-kind image that market leaders so carefully cultivate. After viewing a comparative advertisement, some consumers may associate the two brands involved and believe that they are in some sense substitutes. There is also the possibility that some consumers will believe the message and try the advertiser's brand. The viewers most susceptible to this effect are consumers of the victim's product, the ones who see their regular brand lose.

Thus comparative advertising gives the new or small brand an efficient way to tap into the market segment that the market leader has already carved out. Campaigns like Martinson Decaffeinated versus Sanka, Avis versus Hertz, American Motors versus GM, Goodrich versus Goodyear, and the comparative campaigns I have mentioned are all sponsored by newer or smaller brands. Comparative advertising is an aggressive strategy.

The victim of a comparative ad, then, is likely to be a leading brand in the market, a brand that has invested much time and money in developing a good image and a secure consumer franchise. Such a brand can suffer great damage in a comparative campaign.

What's a victim to do? It can start by asking the following five questions. Then it can decide whether to stand and fight or to grin and bear it.

1 Did anyone actually compare anything?

If Brand A claims that Y% of consumers prefer A to B, one might reasonably think that Brand A gathered together a group of consumers, made them compare Brand A and Brand B, and asked their preferences. But such is not always the case. Using poor research and ingenious circumlocutions, advertisers sometimes make preference claims based on no one comparing anything. Two cases illustrate the technique.

At the height of the Pepsi Challenge, Coca-Cola counterattacked with the claim that New Yorkers prefer Coke to Pepsi two to one. How could two brands simultaneously have a majority of consumers preferring each? While Pepsi had based its claim of consumer preference on taste test surveys, Coke had based its claim on market share. Even market share is subject to interpretation, though. In take-home sales, Coke and Pepsi had roughly equal shares of the New York market, but Coke had a two-to-one advantage when fountain sales were counted.[1] Market share is not the same thing as brand preference. A brand's share reflects factors like order of market entry, advertising effort, marketing acumen, and scale of production.

In a TV commercial for the shampoo called Body on Tap, a high-fashion model says, "In shampoo tests with over 900 women like me, Body on Tap got higher ratings than Prell for body, higher than Flex for conditioning, and higher than Sassoon for strong, healthy looking hair."

Hearing this, one might think that 900 women compared these four shampoos and judged Body on Tap preferable on all three attributes. Not so. The 900 women mentioned in the copy were in fact four groups of about 225 each, and each group had used only one shampoo. Each woman rated 27 attributes of the shampoo she used. The ad copy reflects the attributes for which Body on Tap received higher ratings than at least one other brand. In this survey, no one actually compared anything.[2]

The Body on Tap case is an example of the "blind monadic" survey. The products are unlabeled, making the test "blind," but each subject evaluates only one brand. The blind monadic is a common product test format and is useful for evaluating the relative strengths of various product formulations. But in most cases, the results of a blind monadic test do not sufficiently substantiate a preference claim.

Whenever possible, companies should substantiate comparative ad claims with comparative product tests. Each subject should compare both brands and express a preference. Comparative tests should be blind so that brand names and labeling do not influence the results.

For products like medicines and shampoos, comparing two brands at one sitting is impossible. In these situations, the "staggered monadic" test is a reasonable approach to take. Subjects use each brand once but on two separate occasions and then give their judgments. One way or another, subjects surveyed to support a comparative ad claim should sample both brands and express a preference.

If your brand is victimized and the data that support the comparative claim have been gathered through a monadic product test, you're in luck. You may be able to win a court injunction against the ads. Sassoon stopped the Body on Tap campaign in this way, and the monadic nature of the supporting survey was one of the reasons for the injunction. The comparative advertiser that supports its claim with a monadic product test must have a good reason for not using a comparative format. Products like medicines are not conducive to comparative tests, but even a staggered monadic test requires that subjects eventually sample both products.

2 Who participated in the product test?

The validity of polls resulting in claims like "more people prefer Pepsi to Coke" depends on how well the sample chosen represents the population. The most direct way to gather a representative sample is to use a technique called simple random sampling, in which all members of the target population have a statistically equal chance of inclusion.

For example, consider Riunite, the best-selling imported wine, which is aimed at first-time consumers, who tend to prefer sweet, light, fruity wines. It contains less alcohol than most wines and is marketed to compete with beer and soda as well as other wine brands.[3] The outcome of a preference test between Riunite and, say, Lafite-Rothschild 1975 Bordeaux would depend almost entirely on the sampling procedure employed. If the sample subjects were collected in a college dormitory, Riunite might be preferred, but if the sample consisted of a group of patrons at a fine restaurant, the Lafite would probably be the victor.

The Body on Tap case underscores the point. Body on Tap, so called because it contains beer, is popular with teenagers and at the time of the campaign was intended to penetrate the mature woman market. The victims of the ad—Prell, Flex, and Sassoon—were all established in that segment. The high-fashion model who said that tests were performed on women "like me" was obviously not a teenager.

Yet one-third of the women in the supporting product test were between 13 and 18 years old—

The brief history of comparative ads

Once taboo, comparative advertising became a legitimate practice after the Federal Trade Commission began to advocate its use in 1972. The FTC reasoned that the direct comparison of brands provides more information to consumers and thereby increases competition among producers. And it maintained that those who discourage or forbid direct brand comparisons inhibit free trade by restricting the flow of pertinent product information. The television networks cooperated by lifting their long-standing bans on comparative ads. Advertisers who had previously had to content themselves with labeling the competition "Beep" and "Brand X" could finally call their competitors by name.

Some of the companies involved – especially the large advertising agencies and their larger clients – did not relish the prospect of comparative advertising because it provided too much temptation for mudslinging and name-calling. Grossly inaccurate statements were bound to be made and – worse yet – publicly contested. The commotion would erode the credibility of advertising and sully the reputations of many advertisers. Those most likely to suffer would be the market's leading brands that were apt to be included (that is, "victimized") in someone else's comparative ad.

The networks too were understandably less than enthusiastic about comparative advertising. Their lot was to be the initial arbitrator of comparative claims, to decide which ads were to be aired and which not. Consequently, they would have to maintain costly staffs of lawyers and other experts. And, in denying some claims and allowing others, the networks would be bound to create ill will among their clients. Everyone who had worked to make advertising a reputable gentlemen's activity was unenthusiastic about the change.

In retrospect, we can see that their fears were not unfounded. Comparative advertising, with its attendant litigation and negative publicity, can be seen as hurting the whole advertising profession, according to William Tankersley, former president of the Council of Better Business Bureaus. "The plethora of comparative ads," he has said, "has further damaged the credibility of advertising with equally negative effects on the mores of civilized business behavior."[*] This loss of credibility may be diluting the effect of all advertising. Litigation is very costly. And, most important, it is not clear that comparative advertising has given consumers any more information than they had in the days of Brand X. The dubious benefits of comparative advertising are perhaps best expressed by Tracy Weston, an early advocate of the technique and formerly of the FTC. When asked how comparative advertising has helped consumers, Weston replied, "Confusion is a higher state of knowledge than ignorance."[†]

---

[*] See "Comparative Ads Graded 'F' by CBBB President," *Advertising Age*, October 17, 1977, p. 2.

[†] "It Pays to Knock Your Competitor," *Fortune*, February 13, 1978, p. 104.

members of Body on Tap's segment. So the sample was neither representative of the target segment nor consistent with the model in the ad. Further, the bias in the sampling procedure – the inclusion of a substantial proportion of teenagers – favored Body on Tap.

When confronted with a comparative ad, the victim's manager should ask: "How well does the sample of consumers in the ad represent my target population?" To answer this question, the manager has to know the sampling procedure used to gather the subjects and the composition of the sample. Standard product test sampling procedures are often not adequate. For instance, in recent court cases, use of recruits found at a shopping mall as a sample has not always been judged sufficient for supporting comparative ad claims.[4] For a comparative claim to be unassailable, the sample used to support the claim must be representative of the victim's market segment.

Once managers know their brand is being victimized, they should examine their customer profile and compare it with the sample used to support the competitor's claim. If the sample differs from the customer profile and the difference affects the results of the claim, grounds may exist for a successful challenge.

---

3   Did you measure preference or choice?

When subjects choose between A and B on a blind comparative test, do they state a preference? Sometimes they do, but there's no guarantee. Consider a participant in the Super Bowl Schlitz versus Michelob contest. If he tastes both beers and can't perceive any difference between them, will he admit that he can't in front of millions of TV viewers? Of course not. He will choose one beer rather than the other even though he finds them indistinguishable from each other.

Subjects who do paired comparisons ("Taste A once; taste B once; state your preference") make choices, but these choices can reflect either preference or random guessing. For example, if 100 subjects do a paired comparison and 50 choose Cola A while 50 choose Cola B, there are two possible explanations. Each brand might enjoy a 50% preference share – if subjects can discriminate. But the sample outcome could just as well result from random guessing because nondiscriminating subjects choose either brand with a probability of one-half. So to ascertain subjects' preferences between A and B, we must either assume they can discriminate or we must measure their ability to do so.

One approach to measuring discrimination is to have subjects take a "triangle test" along with a paired comparison test. In a triangle test, subjects taste three product samples (two As and a B or vice versa) and try to identify the one sample that differs from the other two. If our 100 subjects perform correctly on an accompanying triangle test, we can reasonably conclude that their paired comparison choices reflect preferences. But if, say, only a third of our subjects are correct (the proportion expected to guess correctly), their paired comparison choices are not preferences at all but random choices.

Another way to measure discrimination ability is to have subjects do a second paired comparison with the same two brands. If subjects can discriminate and if their preferences are consistent, their choices on the two trials will also be consistent. That is, subjects who choose A on the first paired comparison will choose A on the second and so on. If the subjects do not discriminate, their choices on the two trials will not be correlated. This technique is called consistent preference discrimination testing.

Many preference claims in comparative ads are based only on single paired comparison product tests, so the subjects' discrimination ability has not been tested. These claims include the Pepsi Challenge and the Schlitz versus Michelob, Triumph versus Merit cigarettes, and Sprite versus 7-Up contests. The results reported in some of these campaigns are suspiciously close to a random 50-50 split. How do we know that these campaigns are reporting preferences and not simply random choices? We don't.

While several comparative ads have been based on reported preference results that look suspiciously close to random choice, none has been challenged on this ground. The reason is simple: the victims have been market leaders and reluctant to admit that their products are indistinguishable from newer, smaller, or cheaper brands. To do so would defeat their other marketing efforts.

Yet a victim may be able to respond effectively to a preference claim substantiated with chance results if a product test can be conducted showing that consumers in the victim's segment can discriminate between the two brands in question and that the majority prefer the victim to the challenger. In such a situation, the victim may attribute the challenger's results to an improper sampling procedure.

To my knowledge, no preference claim has ever been stopped because the advertiser failed to show that subjects could discriminate. There are, however, grounds for doing so. The comparative advertising guidelines of the networks and those of the AAAA state that comparative ads cannot be used to extol trivial differences between products. But if most consumers can't discriminate between the two brands in an ad, any differences between them must be trivial. In challenging such preference claims, one could argue that comparative claims supported by blind preference

tests are inappropriate and should not be allowed. Therefore, to be unassailable, a claim that Y% of consumers prefer A to B should be supported by data showing that most consumers in the appropriate market segment can discriminate between them. Anything less is mere chance.

4 Are you inducing parity?

Less expensive brands often claim that they are in some sense as good as the market leader but cost less. The popular Meister Brau campaign—"tastes as good as Bud but at a better price"—is a typical parity claim.

What is parity? Technically speaking, two brands may be at parity in three situations:

Subjects cannot discriminate between two brands.

Subjects can discriminate but have no preference for one or the other.

Subjects can discriminate, but half prefer Brand A and half prefer Brand B.

In each case, neither brand can be said to dominate the other. They are at parity. An advertiser who makes a parity claim must substantiate it with a product test whose results reflect a parity condition.

Probably the most important way to induce such results is through subject selection. If the subjects selected for the survey have little ability to discriminate—say, for example, they are all light users or nonusers of the product class and consequently insensitive to small differences in formulation—the two brands will appear to be at parity.

Another approach is to use a parity-inducing product test design. In one recent case, an advertiser wanted to show that no discrimination existed between product A and product B. The parity test used to support the claim consisted of four paired comparisons, as follows:

First paired comparison	AB
Second paired comparison	AA
Third paired comparison	BA
Fourth paired comparison	BB

The subjects were told: "On each trial, you will taste two samples. They may be different or identical. If they are different, state your preference. If they are identical, say so." Subjects were classified as "discriminators" if they chose the same formulation (that is, A both times or B both times) for the two trials in which the product samples were different *and* if they indicated no difference between the product samples for the two trials in which the samples were the same.

So, to be a discriminator, a subject had to: (1) detect the difference in preparations on two out of two trials, (2) confirm the identity of preparations on two out of two trials, and (3) consistently prefer one preparation to the other. It is easy to see that a complex test like this is much more stringent than, say, a single triangle test ("Which one is different from the other two?"). It is, therefore, much more likely to yield a result consistent with the condition of no discrimination in the population. Parity is induced by the complex test design and stringent discrimination criteria.

"In-home testing" can also induce parity results. Suppose subjects are each given two six-packs of beer (one of Brand A and one of Brand B) to consume over two weeks. They may be instructed to consume all of A and then B, or they may be asked to alternate between them. At the end of two weeks, the subjects state their preferences. At first glance, this appears to be a realistic test because subjects evaluate the two beers in the real world, not the laboratory.

But remember that many situational factors vary during a test. Subjects may consume some bottles at night, some at lunch, some with friends, some alone, and so on. These factors will influence subjects' perceptions and preferences. Thus when in-home testing is used, many factors besides the products themselves influence preference. If these factors vary randomly, as they probably do, they constitute a "noise" that obscures the subjects' preferences. Note, too, that the subjects never sit down and compare the beers side by side and that, in stating their preferences, subjects must remember how they liked beers consumed up to two weeks before. The result is that subjects are less likely to form reliable preferences for either formulation. Judging the beers after the two-week period, half the subjects are likely to choose A randomly and the other half to choose B randomly.

A parity claim should be substantiated with a test that is very sensitive to deviations from parity. If subjects can discriminate and preferences are not evenly split, the product test results should so indicate. In statistical terms, a parity claim is a null hypothesis, and in statistics, it is a well-known fact that null hypotheses are almost impossible to prove. That is, we cannot prove the null hypothesis; we can only show that the data are not inconsistent with the null hypothesis.

For a parity claim, what's desired is "a powerful test" of the parity null hypothesis. The power of a parity test is the probability that it will reject the null hypothesis when it isn't true. If we do a powerful parity test and do not reject the null hypothesis, we

Exhibit	**Results of a blind test comparing Triumph with Merit nonmenthol cigarettes**	
		Percent of sample
Triumph is...	Much better tasting than Merit.	14 %
	Somewhat better tasting than Merit.	22
	About the same in taste as Merit.	24
	Somewhat worse tasting than Merit.	29
	Much worse tasting than Merit.	11

Source:
Jon Zoler, "Research Requirements for
Ad Claims Substantiation,"
Journal of Advertising Research,
April-May 1983, p. 9.

can at least be fairly sure that the null hypothesis is not very *untrue*.

How does one design a powerful parity test? Here are three suggestions:

1   Whenever possible, substantiate a parity claim with a comparative test in which subjects judge products side by side. This is how small differences in formulation become most noticeable.

2   If the parity claim is one of no discrimination, use a very simple discrimination test. Test complexity should be no reason for apparent nondiscrimination. Under many plausible conditions, the simple triangle test provides a good way to evaluate the no-discrimination null hypothesis.

3   Add subjects to the parity test to increase its power. The larger the sample, the more powerful the test. Adding subjects costs a lot, but compared with the cost of litigation, subjects are a bargain.

What does all this mean for the victim of a parity claim? If the victim suspects that a shoddy product test is the substantiation of the challenger's parity claim, the proper course of action is clear: the victim should perform a powerful test of the parity null hypothesis. The null hypothesis will probably be rejected with a high degree of confidence. If a parity hypothesis is not true, disproving it is fairly easy. All it takes is the proper product test design and enough subjects.

5   Is your claim consistent with the test results?

That "Triumph beats Merit" was the claim in a recent comparative campaign. The explanation? "An amazing 60% said that 3-milligram Triumph tastes as good as or better than 8-milligram Merit." In the product test used to support the claim, subjects were asked to rate the Triumph cigarette along a five-point scale ranging from "much better tasting than Merit" to "much worse tasting." The survey results are shown in the *Exhibit.*

True to the claim, 60% of those polled said that Triumph tasted as good as or better than Merit. But the *Exhibit* shows that 11% of the sample said that Triumph was "much worse tasting," 29% said it was "somewhat worse tasting," and 24% said it was "about the same." Adding these up, we find that an even more amazing 64% of the subjects said that Merit tasted as good as or better than Triumph. Did Triumph really beat Merit?

Philip Morris, the producer of Merit, obtained an injunction against this ad. The grounds for the injunction deserve comment. The copy in the Triumph ad is not literally false. In fact, 60% of those polled said that Triumph tasted as good as or better than Merit, but given the way the subjects' votes were counted, it's not clear that Triumph beat Merit. Philip Morris conducted a communications test of the ad copy. That is, by having subjects answer questions about the ad, Philip Morris investigators tried to ascertain what the Triumph ad was really saying to consumers. They found that, to 37% of the smokers who saw the ad, the statement "Triumph beats Merit" meant "Triumph was better tasting than Merit." This impression is counter to the results in the *Exhibit,* and because of the finding that the ad conveyed an incorrect impression, the ad was enjoined.

In translating a favorable product test outcome into a claim, comparative advertisers tend to state results in the strongest possible way. Indeed, the language used in the copy sometimes connotes a stronger image of the results than may be the case, even though the language itself is not literally false. But to stand up in court, the copy in the ad cannot just be literally consistent with the results of the substantiating survey; it must also give the correct total impression. To be more exact, the copy cannot convey an incorrect impression to a large portion of the viewing audience.

If the copy does convey such an impression, the victim may be able to have the ad enjoined under federal law. As with the examples previously cited, the process by which the victim can do so includes two steps: first, a communications test to determine what the ad is saying to viewers and second, a demonstration that a large proportion of the viewers is retaining an impression that is inconsistent with the results of the supporting product test.

How should you respond?

If the comparative advertiser can answer all five of these questions satisfactorily, the ad is at least reasonably well substantiated. In such cases, a challenge of the comparative claim is risky because if the challenge is unsuccessful, the victim may incur much negative publicity for no gain. Certainly, Coke's interests were not served by the dogfight that followed the Pepsi Challenge. And McDonald's unsuccessful contentions about Burger King's comparative ads probably actually enhanced Burger King's campaign. Fighting a comparative claim—especially in the public arena—should be done only when the chances of winning are reasonably good.

If the comparative advertiser stumbles over one or more of these questions and the claim is poorly grounded, the victim should contest the ad. There are several avenues to take.

The networks

If a televised claim is particularly shoddy, the quickest redress is to protest directly to the television networks. To evaluate advertising claims, the networks maintain broadcast standards departments, staffed with lawyers and editorial writers who are charged with keeping false and deceptive ads off the air. If a network's broadcast standards department has already approved a claim, getting it pulled off may be problematic. Still, a victim can usually get a fair hearing. The great virtue of this alternative is that it is inexpensive and, when successful, very quick.

NAD

The National Advertising Division of the Council of Better Business Bureaus hears protests from victims. But because its decisions are not binding and because NAD cannot force an advertiser to make its substantiation data available for the victim's examination, NAD is a reasonable recourse only if both victim and advertiser are willing to cooperate and adhere to the ruling. And because of the maneuvering of victim and advertiser, response from NAD can sometimes be maddeningly slow. Cases can linger in review for months, sometimes long after the advertiser has decided on its own to stop using the offending claim.

NARB

Some advertisers and victims that are dissatisfied with NAD rulings take their cases to the National Advertising Review Board, which is jointly sponsored by the Council of Better Business Bureaus, the American Association of Advertising Agencies, the Association of National Advertisers, and the American Advertising Federation. NARB often acts as an appellate court to NAD. Since it is also an industry-sponsored arbitrator, NARB is subject to some of the same limitations as NAD. That is, the cooperation and compliance of both the advertiser and the victim are required for an NARB review to be effective.

The FTC

A victim can protest to the Federal Trade Commission, but especially recently, the FTC has shied away from such cases. While the FTC has long encouraged comparative advertising as a benefit to consumers, the agency appears to be untroubled by the battles that this encouragement has ignited among producers. Moreover, the FTC's primary mandate is to protect the consumer, not the comparative advertising victim. Therefore, when protesting to the FTC, the victim must show that a misleading comparative claim is injuring the consumer. Proving that consumers are being adversely affected is often more difficult than showing that the product tests do not support the claim. Finally, the FTC has limited resources, and proceedings can take months or even years.

The Lanham Act

Perhaps the quickest, most effective relief from an offensive comparative claim comes through Section 43(a) of the Lanham Act, which prohibits "any false description or representation . . . of any good or service." This statute was first applied to comparative advertising in the 1976 case of *American Home Products* v. *Johnson & Johnson* (Anacin versus Tylenol). Since then, numerous victims have tried to stop comparative ads by filing for injunction in federal court under this act. Recent cases include *Carter-Wallace* v. *Johnson & Johnson, Reynolds* v. *Lorillard, Quaker State* v. *Burmah Castrol*, and the Triumph and Body on Tap cases mentioned previously.

Court proceedings can be costly but have several attractive features. First, the victim does not have to prove that the ad is injuring the consumer.

Instead, the victim need only show that the ad is likely to cause damage to the victim's own sales—usually an easier task. Second, by filing for an injunction, the victim can get quick access to the claim substantiation data, even without the advertiser's consent. Third, court rulings are binding; if the court rules in favor of the victim, the ad must be pulled out or the claim modified. Last, and probably most important from the standpoint of the victim, recourse to the courts under the Lanham Act is fast. Cases are usually decided after several days or weeks. For these reasons, filing for injunction under the Lanham Act has become the avenue many victims take.

Comparative ads are now commonplace, accounting for 35% of all television advertising.[5] The victims of these comparative ads suffer sales loss and image deterioration. Managers can no longer afford to remain ignorant of product testing as it is used in comparative advertising. The stakes are too high. At the very least, managers must know the right questions to ask.

References

1 See Nancy Giges, "Comparative Ads: Battles That Wrote Dos and Don'ts," *Advertising Age*, September 29, 1980, p. 59.

2 See Sidney A. Diamond, "Market Research Latest Target in Ad Claims," *Advertising Age*, January 25, 1982, p. 52.

3 Adapted from David L. Kurtz and Louis E. Boone, *Marketing* (New York: Dryden Press, 1984), pp. 17-18.

4 See Robert G. Sugarman, "Recent Developments in Advertising Litigation," *Marketing Review*, November-December 1980, p. 23.

5 See "More Firms File Challenges to Rivals' Comparative Ads," *Wall Street Journal*, January 12, 1984.

Reprint 85404

Advertising Techniques

Ideas for Action

Developments, trends & useful proposals for the attention of managers

Edited by
Timothy B. Blodgett

Research on advertising techniques that work – and don't work

David Ogilvy and
Joel Raphaelson

Mr. Ogilvy is the creative head of Ogilvy & Mather, the advertising agency. He wrote the well-known book, Confessions of an Advertising Man. *Mr. Raphaelson is senior vice president of Ogilvy & Mather and executive creative director of its Chicago office.*

Marketers devote much research to positioning their products, defining their target audiences, and selecting the benefits they promise in their advertising.

Once they have settled these matters of strategy, they usually give the creative people in their advertising agencies wide latitude in deciding matters of execution. Thus, the marketers take a livelier interest in what to say than in how to say it. They assume that, if the strategy is correct, the battle is more than half won; the rest is detail.

But if the execution is inept, nobody pays attention to the commercials or reads the advertisements. You can't save souls in an empty church.

Some 85% of magazine readers do not remember seeing the average advertisement, and 75% of viewers cannot recall the average television commercial the day after they have seen it. There can be little doubt that if more advertisements were better executed, these appalling figures would be reduced.

Advertising could achieve better results if more people who create it would take the trouble to learn which techniques are most likely to work. By techniques we mean such things as slice-of-life demonstrations in television commercials and before-and-after comparisons in print advertising.

Why doesn't the advertising community take the trouble to study the evidence? Creative people rely on intuition and on tests of individual commercials. As a rule, advertisers and agencies do not *accumulate* their test scores and analyze them to learn which techniques work best. Marketers can stimulate a more scientific attitude.

When George Gallup was at Young & Rubicam in the 1930s, he not only measured the readership of individual magazine advertisements but also categorized them by the techniques used. He reported average scores, technique by technique. Applying his findings, Vaughn Flannery and others at Young & Rubicam created advertisements that got significantly higher readership than those of other agencies.

After he started Gallup & Robinson, Gallup continued this analysis. Mills Shepard conducted similar analyses for *McCall's* magazine, and Harold Sykes of the American Newspaper Publishers Association did the same thing for newspaper ads. In 1947 Harold Rudolph published his book, *Attention and Interest Factors in Advertising.* (His observation that "story appeal" in illustrations attracts above-average attention led to the eyepatch for the man in the Hathaway shirt.)

But about 25 years ago the advertising community lost interest in analyzing factors, much to the joy of the lunatic fringe of creative people in agencies who abhor any research that challenges their pretensions to omniscience.

We maintain that it is important to collect information on positive and negative factors. When we study research firms' analyses of their accumulated scores, we are impressed by how little the major findings have changed over the years. With rare exceptions, consumers continue to react to the same stimuli in the same ways.

Television commercials

The findings we report for television come principally from Mapes & Ross, a research firm whose measurements include a rating for a commercial's ability to change brand preference. We attach importance to this measurement because of its high correlation with performance in the marketplace.

The firm correlated the purchase behavior of TV viewers with their responses to questions about 142 commercials in 55 product categories, asked over a five-month period. (The commercials promoted no new brands or "big ticket" items.) Viewers who reported a change in brand preference bought the advertised product 3.3 times more often than viewers who did not report such a change.

Another analysis covered 809 commercials – for food products, appliances, apparel, and five other broad categories. When measured for their ability to change brand preference, the following techniques scored above average:

1   Problem solution.

2   Humor (when the humor is pertinent to the selling proposition).

3   Relevant characters (personalities, developed by the advertising, who become associated with a brand).

4   Slice-of-life (enactments in which a doubter is converted).

5   News (new products, new uses, new ideas, new information).

6   Candid camera testimonials.

7   Demonstrations.

On the average, commercials built around celebrities were not notably successful in changing brand preference; 21% fewer consumers reported a change in preference influenced by celebrity commercials, compared with the average change for all commercials studied. However, when measured for viewers' ability to *recall* a commercial 24 hours after seeing it, celebrity commercials scored well above average: 22% more respondents.

Why this difference of −21 to +22 between brand preference and recall? We suspect it is because many such messages focus attention on the celebrity rather than on the product.

Creative people sometimes resist this kind of factor analysis, partly because they misunderstand it. We do not hold that, for example, every slice-of-life commercial will change more brand preferences than every

celebrity commercial. We say that the *average* number of brand preferences changed by slice-of-life commercials is markedly higher than the *average* number changed by celebrity commercials.

Accordingly, all other things being equal, a copywriter who wishes to change a viewer's preference toward the particular brand is more likely to succeed with the slice-of-life technique than with a celebrity. Of course, all other things are not always equal. Some products do not lend themselves to slice-of-life. A few have won fame and fortune from long association with a celebrity.

But a skillful craftsman, in advertising as in any other trade, benefits from knowing that he or she is swimming downstream by employing some techniques and upstream by employing others. One should not jump into the water without knowing which way the current is flowing.

Here are some more techniques, commonly used in television commercials, that score above or below average:

Cartoons and animation are effective with children but below average with grownups.

Commercials with a lot of very short scenes and many changes of situation are below average.

"Supers" (words on the screen) add to a commercial's power to change brand preference. But the words must reinforce the main point.

Commercials that do not show the package, or that end without the brand name, are below average in changing brand preference.

Commercials that start with the key idea stand a better chance of holding attention and persuading the viewer. When you advertise fire extinguishers, open with the fire.

We also have reason to believe that commercials with unusual casting – character actors rather than bland stereotypes – perform conspicu-

ously above average in their ability to change brand preference. And visual devices that stick in the mind's eye, sometimes called mnemonic, increase brand identification when repeated over a long period.

Magazine advertisements

Most studies of print advertising measure its ability to attract attention, to get read, and to stick in the memory. For nearly half a century, Gallup, Starch, and other research firms have measured the noting and readership of tens of thousands of advertisements.

Nobody has been able to correlate these measurements with sales, but it is reasonable to assume that an advertisement that people notice is more effective than one they pass by; that it is better if your ad is read thoroughly than if it is only glanced at; and that it is better still if readers can remember something of what they read.

We have found that:

As in television, ads with news score above average.

Injecting "story appeal" into illustrations increases chances of attracting attention – vide the eyepatch.

Before-and-after illustrations score above average.

It pays to show the product in use and the end result of having used it.

"Blind" headlines that require reading of the body copy to decipher them don't work well. Copywriters who believe they can tease readers into an advertisement are throwing money away.

Long headlines – 13 words or more – usually work better than short ones.

Headlines that quote somebody, in quotation marks, score dramatically high – 28%

above the average for all headlines recalled, according to one study.

Here is a headline that quotes an engineer. It also contains many words (17), news, brand name, and consumer benefit: "At Sixty Miles an Hour, the Loudest Noise in This New Rolls-Royce Comes from the Electric Clock."

We wish we could report which factors work best in radio and posters. We have been unable to find enough reliable data to lead us to any firm conclusions.

Role of emotion

The findings we have reported apply particularly to the kind of advertising in which an appeal to reason is an important element. This does not deny the importance of *emotion* in nearly all advertising.

Few purchases of any kind are made for entirely rational reasons. Even a purely functional product such as laundry detergent may offer what is now called an "emotional end benefit"— say, the satisfaction of seeing one's children in bright, clean clothes. In some product categories the rational element is small. These include soft drinks, beer, cosmetics, certain personal-care products, and most fashion products. And who hasn't experienced the surge of joy that accompanies the purchase of a new car?

It also pays to use an emotional approach, particularly in television, when a product does not differ significantly from its competitors.

How best to appeal to the emotions is beyond the scope of this article.

Resistance from creative people

There are two *wrong* ways to react to this information. One is to clutch it as a magic formula for success. The other, more common, way is to reject it as an inhibition to creativity. Here are the reasons creative people give for rejecting it, followed by our observations:

"The creative process cannot be reduced to a set of rules." We do not try to impose this information as rules. We only report on how most consumers react, most of the time, to different stimuli.

"The best advertising arises from the creative person's instinct and intuition, not from formulae." We are at pains to tell our creative colleagues that, while knowledge of positive and negative factors will help them avoid egregious mistakes, it is no substitute for the invention of Big Ideas. And these are the product of the unconscious.

"Some of the most successful campaigns go against the averages." This is true. But it leads to a fault in reasoning—the doctrine that, since *some* people succeed by going against the averages, the best way to succeed is to go against them. A blind pig may sometimes find truffles, but it helps if he forages in an oak forest.

"Adherence to averages will never result in outstanding work." This is not true. Many successful advertising campaigns come from inspired use of tried-and-true techniques. Above-average techniques do not condemn you to mediocre results. Nor will they guarantee success. But they do improve the chances that you won't waste your money.

We have observed that the best copywriters and art directors study the research, refer to it, and employ it judiciously as one of the most useful tools of their craft. If clients were to support further research along these lines, more creative people would use the findings, and more advertisements would do their jobs.

Reprint 82449

Growing Concerns

Topics of particular interest to owners and managers of smaller businesses

Edited by
David E. Gumpert

Your own brand of advertising for nonconsumer products

Herbert L. Kahn

Heads of smaller organizations who skillfully oversee the exacting manufacture of products like scientific instruments, computers, and office automation systems may hesitate to contribute to their advertising. Presenting products to the customer in an appealing way is to such people an inexact matter that is usually best left to the advertising experts.

More often than not, though, these managers are themselves the true experts at advertising complex nonconsumer products. They are the ones who have the technical expertise to explain their products effectively. Like their customers, these managers have backgrounds in science, engineering, or finance. What they see as a shortcoming can be an advertising boon.

Mr. Kahn is a high-tech marketing consultant and president of Market Analysis Research Systems Company in Weston, Massachusetts. At Perkin-Elmer Corporation and Instrumentation Laboratory, Inc., he has been responsible for the economic health of many complex nonconsumer products.

Managers of small and medium-sized companies or divisions that make complex nonconsumer products are often uncomfortable with the responsibility of advertising them. These are products that require an effort to understand – products like scientific instruments, computers, software, advanced materials, production machinery, and office automation systems. Most of these managers have training in science, engineering, or finance and prefer to deal with measurements and calculations. A nonnumerical area like advertising is to them a murky field lit up spasmodically by flashes of genius and uncertain in results. They are tempted to yield the ground to specialized departments and agencies, staffed by people who presumably understand such things.

These managers are making a mistake. They forget how much money goes into advertising and how much information the sales literature for such sophisticated products needs. A company usually spends about 3% of its gross on promotion, including literature and trade shows. If a business has revenues of $20 million a year, that's $600,000!

Ads in printed media account for a third of that. Rarely do people in advertising have the technical knowledge to write them, let alone make advertising policy or originate advertising campaigns for these products. Just as war "is much too serious a matter to be entrusted to the military," as French statesman Georges Clemenceau once said, so advertising is much too important to be left to advertising specialists.

Be aware of the measurement quandary

To be sure, the results of advertising are uncertain. Measuring its effectiveness is nearly impossible.

Everyone knows that it is more difficult to measure human reactions than, say, to count up inventory. Nevertheless, advertising professionals feel pressed to do more than merely ask the client for faith in their services. They have devised some systems to measure advertising effectiveness, many of which seem logical, some of which seem convincing, and all of which can be used to produce computer printouts that give an air of rationality to the subject. Most systems of this kind are less useful than they appear.

Can you measure the value of an ad by the number of sales leads it brings you – that is, by the number of people who circle the reader's service number? Well, if you want thousands of sales leads, you can design the ad to provide them. Just offer a free piece of tutorial literature – say, a 16-page booklet entitled "Digital Computers Simply Explained." Free articles always draw a big response. Add a sentence saying that anyone circling the number will participate in a random drawing for a VCR, and you'll get an even greater response. Without the use of such scurvy tricks, the number of sales leads you get may depend more on the interest and newness of the product than on the skill of presentation, unless the ad is so poor as to be incomprehensible.

You can measure what proportion of the readers of an ad notice or remember it. But can you establish a link between the memorability of an ad and the number of people buying the product? Not really. To score high, illustrate the ad with a photo of an owl flying away with a baby. Everybody will notice and remember the owl but not necessarily buy the product.

How about measuring the effectiveness of an ad by finding out what percentage of its viewers read the ad all the way through? If the entire text of the ad is "Our machine is number one," everybody who starts will finish, but will anyone know enough about the product to be impressed by it?

If none of these points is convincing, perhaps the bottom line will be. Recently, a company spent a lot of money on advertising with a certain agency. For three years, sales doubled and profits tripled. But why? Because of the advertising? Or despite the advertising? Or was the advertising performance irrelevant to the result? There's no sure way of telling.

Don't leave it to the experts

If you can't measure the effectiveness of advertising, isn't that an argument for leaving it in the hands of professionals? For both financial and psychological reasons, the answer is no.

First, the products we are talking about are complex and specialized. Before such a product can be intelligently advertised, the people writing the ads must understand its function, its operating principles, and its advantages and disadvantages. They must know what its competition is and who its customers are. In other words, this kind of promotion requires a great deal of attention and expertise.

An advertising agency can employ no more than three people for every million dollars' worth of billing. A $200,000 account can command about 60% of a person-year—that is, 60% of the time of one person or 20% of the time of three people. Whichever way the agency divides the effort, its people cannot take the time to learn everything they need to know about a complex, low-volume product in order to create useful advertising for it, even if their backgrounds qualify them to do so.

Second, psychology compounds the issue. The glamour area of

advertising is not high technology but consumer products. Most advertising professionals bring to high-tech advertising an attitude that is appropriate for promoting consumer products, even though the problems are entirely different. They study and admire the techniques that consumer advertisers use to draw attention to basically uninteresting, easily understood, and marginally differentiated commodities such as toothpaste, aspirin, and soft drinks. Ads for these products run in media where they have to compete with subjects that go to the root of human experience, such as love, death, and basketball. Ad agency people may therefore believe that the nonconsumer product is also uninteresting and that they must spice up its presentation in every possible way.

Choose the right approach

Advertising complex industrial products is actually easier than promoting most consumer goods. For one thing, the potential user of complex products finds them interesting and actually wants to learn about them, provided that the information is not too obscure to read through. For another, the ads appear in media where there is not much competition from editorial material. Instead of running next to color photographs of "the Roommate of the Year," the high-tech ad may abut an article entitled "Temperature of Platform, Wall, and Vapor in a Pulse-heated Electrothermal Graphite Furnace"—simply not such stuff as dreams are made on.

Manufacturers of nonconsumer goods must show advertising professionals how the approach to promoting these products differs from that for consumer items because the realization does not come automatically. Being nontechnical, advertising pros are likely to regard numerically controlled milling machines as even more boring than laundry detergents and will have difficulty imagining that customers virtually lust after them. The people from the advertising agency will probably not read, and certainly not understand, the journals in which the high-tech ads will appear.

Avoid two mistakes

To produce successful ads for complex nonconsumer products, the company's marketers and the advertising professionals must work closely together, with mutual respect for each other's areas of expertise. Moreover (this ought to be obvious but seems not to be), everybody involved should believe that what an ad says is important.

Their teamwork can prevent two flaws that are common in high-tech product advertising:

1   Defeating the customer's effort to read the text by trying to make an ad "stand out" with "interesting" typography. If you look through any technical journal, you will find ads written in script or in simulated graffiti or printed with the lines at 45-degree angles. You'll see odd typefaces and unusual color combinations—say, the text written in green over a photograph of flames.

This approach is not very inviting, in my opinion. From reading books, newspapers, and magazines, people have become used to seeing dark letters on light backgrounds, arranged in paragraphs that proceed in orderly fashion from top to bottom. Any marked deviation from this pattern makes the text difficult to read.

2   Basing the ad on inadequate information so that the text becomes a collection of generalized, boastful sentences that could apply to anything. Such ads occupy space without doing anything useful for either the advertiser or the customer. Customers are busy and will instinctively stop reading empty material. Advertisers presumably have real information to convey and should not waste expensive space with windy generalities.

To be sure you and your advertising people do not produce generic ads, you can apply the "pocketknife rule": if you can replace the subject of a sentence with *pocketknife* without altering the sense, the sentence is generic and should be eliminated. A vintage example of a generic ad appeared in the May 1985 issue of *Laboratory Equipment*, a tabloid monthly for analytical chemists. Here is how the copy read (I have disguised the company's name as *Robinson* and written words like *pocketknife* in parentheses next to the actual subjects):

"Remember the first Robinson spectrophotometer (pocketknife) you used? The simplicity and dependability?

"The tradition continues.

"Behind the simple operation of the new XX Series Spectrophotometers (pocketknives) are technological advances that give these instruments incredible capability.

"They feature full programmability so you have control of all operations....

"And that's that. You save time. You eliminate errors. There are four models available, offering you the choice of scanning (cork screws) or programmability (nail files) or both. All of them deliver the day-in, day-out reliability we built an industry on.

"A utilitarian, functional instrument so simple anyone can run it, so dependable you'll never give it a second thought. And now is the perfect time to find out about it. For more information, contact your Robinson representative...."

Work with the agency

To get the most for their money, how should complex nonconsumer goods managers work with advertising professionals? Not by doing their work for them. As David Ogilvy says in his book *Confessions of an Advertising Man,* "Why keep a dog and bark yourself?"

Management must, however, specify what it wants and decide for itself what the general theme of a campaign is to be. Management must tell the agency who the audience is, which points to stress, and what information to convey. As I have said, it is simply unrealistic to expect the advertising professionals to have enough technical knowledge to make this kind of decision.

Moreover, the company's own marketers should select the journals in which to run the ads, either from their own knowledge or by calling up a few dozen customers and asking them what they read.

The company should, above all, make the advertising pros realize that the customers for these complex products really do want to read about them, provided the text is clear and geared to their interests. The company should not let the agency commit the sin of trying to seduce the customer by writing headlines that pretend to be about something else. The agency should be told: "Be clever if you can, by all means, but if you can't, be factual."

The agency for Hotpack Corporation, a manufacturer of laboratory ovens, seems to have decided that ovens are boring and has produced an ad saying: "The American work ethic is alive and well in Philadelphia." That is information that will warm the hearts of politicians, sociologists, and patriots, but no politicians or sociologists, and only a few patriots, buy laboratory ovens. A better headline would have been: "Hotpack offers ovens with 20-cubic-foot capacity and 0.5-degree accuracy," which, while not brilliant, efficiently conveys the information customers want.

One argument that will never be settled is whether to use long copy or short. Advertising pros usually line up on the side of short copy. It looks better, and it is easier to write (one can write 50 powerful words about a product without even knowing what it is). Because many people hate to read, the pros could in fact be right. But mail-order advertisers, who are the only people who live and die by the results of their ads, almost always use long copy. Think of the mail pieces routinely sent to executives about training courses and the mail-order ads in airline magazines. They all contain many words and very little white space.

Whether the text is long or short, management must insist on its being clear and comprehensible, filled with facts rather than wind, interesting if possible but not cute, and written from the user's viewpoint rather than the manufacturer's or the designer's. Sandy Flandreau, former advertising manager at Perkin-Elmer Corporation, used to train subordinates by teaching them to stress "owner benefits" rather than "good qualities," which he described as design features that the user is unlikely to understand. It is an owner benefit for the blade of a pocketknife to be rust resistant. That it is made of chromium-vanadium steel is a "good

quality"—mainly of interest to other designers of pocketknives.

Advertisers of complex industrial products should leave the fancy graphics, talking dogs, flying teenagers, and punchy slogans to the consumer products people. Sergeant Joe Friday of TV's "Dragnet" program spoke for industrial advertisers when he said, "Just the facts, ma'am." Just the facts, clearly and truthfully presented, give nonconsumer products the best probability of success in the market.

Reprint 86108

READ THE FINE PRINT

REPRINTS
Telephone: 617-495-6192
Fax: 617-495-6985

Current and past articles are available, as is an annually updated index. Discounts apply to large-quantity purchases.

Please send orders to HBR Reprints Harvard Business School Publishing Division Boston, MA 02163.

HOW CAN *HARVARD BUSINESS REVIEW* ARTICLES WORK FOR YOU?

For years, we've printed a microscopically small notice on the editorial credits page of the *Harvard Business Review* alerting our readers to the availability of *HBR* articles.

Now we invite you to take a closer look at some of the many ways you can put this hard-working business tool to work for you.

IN THE CORPORATE CLASSROOM.

There's no more effective, or cost-effective, way to supplement your corporate training programs than in-depth, incisive *HBR* articles.

Affordable and accessible, it's no wonder hundreds of companies and consulting organizations use *HBR* articles as a centerpiece for management training.

IN-BOX INNOVATION.

Where do your company's movers and shakers get their big ideas? Many find the inspiration for innovation in the pages of *HBR*. They then share the wealth and spread the word by distributing *HBR* articles to company colleagues.

IN MARKETING AND SALES SUPPORT.

HBR articles are a substantive leave-behind to your sales calls. And they can add credibility to your direct mail campaigns. They demonstrate that your company is on the leading edge of business thinking.

CREATE CUSTOM ARTICLES.

If you want to pack even greater power in your punch, personalize *HBR* articles with your company's name or logo. And get the added benefit of putting your organization's name before your customers.

AND THERE ARE 500 MORE REASONS IN THE *HBR CATALOG*.

In all, the *Harvard Business Review Catalog* lists articles on over 500 different subjects. Plus, you'll find books and videos on subjects you need to know.

The catalog is yours for just $8.00. To order *HBR* articles or the *HBR Catalog* (No. 21019), call 617-495-6192. Please mention telephone order code 025A when placing your order. Or FAX us at 617-495-6985.

And start putting *HBR* articles to work for you.

Harvard Business School Publications

Call 617-495-6192 to order the *HBR Catalog*.

(Prices and terms subject to change.)